COUNTRY WALKS

D0522998

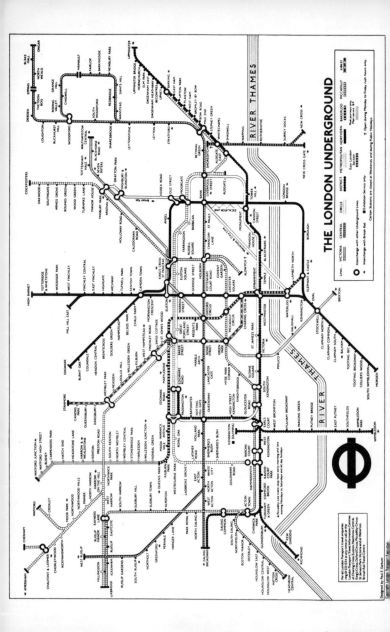

THE LONDON UNDERGROUND

COUNTRY WALKS

*by Leigh Hatts
and Ron Pigram*

LONDON TRANSPORT
55 BROADWAY
LONDON SW1

© London Transport

First Published: April, 1980

ISBN 0 85329 106 3

Printed in Great Britain
by W & J Mackay Limited, Chatham
280/023RP/10M

Foreword

THIS LATEST selection of walks will take you into London's rural corners and all the Home Counties. We have also included an inner London walk that runs through the very heart of the West End parks.

As always there are several circular walks and for more experienced walkers there is a 16 mile challenge to be had by treating the Ongar and Epping walks as one. The books offer a detailed description of more than 100 miles of clear paths which can be enjoyed in winter, autumn and spring as much as the summer – a route repeated in a new season will provide new pleasures.

Care has been taken to make sure that the information given is correct in every detail but paths are sometimes redirected. We always welcome comments from those who experience any difficulty.

Leigh Hatts has surveyed and compiled this edition with the exception of Walks 3 and 4 which were written by Ron Pigram.

Maps were drawn by the London Transport Commercial Drawing Office.

The Country Code

Guard against all risk of fire
Fasten all gates
Keep dogs under proper control
Keep to the paths across farm land
Avoid damaging fences, hedges and walls
Leave no litter – take it home
Safeguard water supplies
Protect wild life, wild plants and trees
Go carefully on country roads
Respect the life of the countryside

LONDON TRANSPORT

Bus and Underground maps, leaflets and bus timetables for individual routes can be obtained free from any London Transport Travel Information Centre (at Charing Cross, Euston, Heathrow Central, King's Cross, Oxford Circus, Piccadilly Circus, and Victoria Underground Stations and Waterloo British Rail Travel Centre). Or write to the Public Relations Officer, London Transport, 55 Broadway, SW1. For telephone Underground, bus and Green Line enquiries, day or night, ring 01–222 1234.

LONDON COUNTRY BUSES

Details of Green Line Coach and London Country Bus services can be obtained from London Country Bus Services, Bell Street, Reigate, Surrey. Telephone 74–42411. (Country Bus and Green Line maps are available free from London Transport Travel Information Centre.)

BRITISH RAIL

Passenger train information can be obtained from the main line stations or by telephone:

Eastern Region	01–283 7171 or 01–837 3355
London Midland Region	01–387 3355
Southern Region	01–928 5100
Western Region	01–262 6767

Every effort is made to ensure that the information given in this book is correct, but details are liable to alteration without notice and London Transport does not accept responsibility for any inaccuracies. The inclusion of a building or open space does not necessarily imply the right of public entry.

CONTENTS

1 Below the Castle

SLOUGH – ETON – ETON WICK – WINDSOR – THE HOME PARK – UPTON
5½ or 8 MILES

THIS WALK wanders beside the Thames and through the countryside which lies between modern Slough and ancient Windsor. The familiar paintings and photographs of the Castle have mostly been inspired by the view from Eton and the Brocas Meadows – Turner came here in about 1829.

SLOUGH: Bus 81. Green Line Coach 701, 704, 726. British Rail.

WINDSOR: Green Line Coach 700 (from Victoria in summer only) 701, 704, 718, 724, 726. British Rail.

SLOUGH was on the Bath Road. St. Mary's, which replaced a neo-Norman building of 1835, was begun in 1876 and completed in 1912. The four tall stained glass windows in the west wall, designed by Alfred A. Walmark in 1915 and the forerunners of modern windows, were given by James Elleman of Elleman's Embrocation. Observatory House in Windsor Road stands on the site of the original Observatory House which was the home of Sir William Herschel, the discoverer of the planet Uranus. He continued his researches here and, as Court Astronomer, entertained the great scientists. In the garden he built his 40-foot telescope and when George III stepped into it he offered his hand, to the hesitant Archbishop of Canterbury, saying 'Come my Lord Bishop, I will show you the way to heaven'. Walking through the telescope became fashionable. Fanny Burney, the Diarist (see also page 80) did it in 1786 'without the least inconvenience'. She could have managed even if she had been dressed 'in feathers and a bell hoop – such is the circumference'. Dr. Johnson's friend, Mrs. Thrale, with amazing foresight, found that through the glass 'the empty craters of the moon (stood) out quite clearly. For my part it gave me the

Idea of a ruined, not a habitable World'. The sculpture, by Franta Belsky, symbolizes the triangular structure of the telescope. Victoria Terrace, on the north and west side of Herschel Park, is said to have been designed by Joseph Paxton, but Benjamin Bank, who worked with Wyatville at Windsor, may have been responsible. The first charity 'flag day' was held on Salt Hill where Eton College boys sold salt to raise money for University expenses – those who agreed to buy were given a flag so that they would not be asked again. Queen Victoria made her first train journey from Slough although Eton College had opposed the idea of a station here. Baylis House, in Stoke Poges Lane, was built about 1695 for the Dean of Windsor. The nearby castellated Horlick's factory was erected in 1908 – the design is based on the firm's building in America.

Leave the High Street and walk down Windsor Road to pass Observatory House (left). Turn left through a gateway to St. Mary's Church. On reaching the church bear right to pass the west doors of St. Mary's and follow a path to Albert Street.

Turn left and follow Albert Street, which becomes Mere Road, to reach a roundabout at Upton (see page 8).

Turn right along Datchet Road to cross the M4. On the far side of the bridge go right to follow a footpath down the bank to reach the end of a road. Follow this road to a bend and turn right by a letterbox. Cross a small bridge and walk through a long avenue of trees to reach a road. Pass through the wooden gateway opposite, cross another bridge, and follow the path. When the way approaches a brick bridge (there is a view of Eton College ahead) bear right and follow a path across a cricket field (known as Upper Club) to reach a gateway by the old 1866 Cricket Pavilion.

Go left along the road to cross a brook (known as 'The Jordan'). On 30 November the annual wall game takes place below the wall on the left. At a road junction there is an ornate wrought iron lamp standard known as the Burning Bush (erected 1864). Most houses in this area belong to Eton College and the main buildings are to the left.

ETON COLLEGE was modelled on Winchester and founded in 1440 by Henry VI, then only 19 years old. 70 poor scholars formed the nucleus of the school and there are still 70 King's Scholars (a title granted by George III) but most of the school consists of 1,100 'Oppidons' who pay full fees. Former pupils include Charles James Fox, the first Duke of Wellington, Shelley, Gladstone (who loved his 'glorious school'), the late Duke of Gloucester, King Leopold of the Belgians, Lord Snowdon and Sir James Goldsmith. On the north side of school yard is Long Chamber which was the principal dormitory up to 1844. In the centre of the Yard there is a statue of Henry VI by Francis Bird. The Cloisters, beyond, date from 1445. The 15th-century Chapel was intended to form only the choir of Eton Church. The paintings on the north wall were whitewashed over during Elizabeth I's reign and finally uncovered in 1923. The game of fives was invented here in the Middle Ages when boys hit a ball against the chapel's outside wall. Today's boys, who all have a room of their own, wear black tail coats in mourning for George III. The historic buildings, including the chapel, are open daily 14 00 (10 30 during holidays) to 17 00, admission 30p, children 10p.

To avoid Eton Wick go ahead up Eton High Street to reach Windsor Bridge (page 6).

Turn right to pass the Burning Bush lamp and enter Common Lane. Ahead is the 18th-century Common Lane House. Keep to the left of Common Lane House to pass Godolphin House (left), which was built as a boarding house in 1722, and Holland House to walk along a walled path known as Judy's Passage. On reaching a modern courtyard turn left and then right on to another enclosed path.

Beyond the gate, at the far end, bear right round the edge of a field and then left (not over the stile) to walk towards the railway

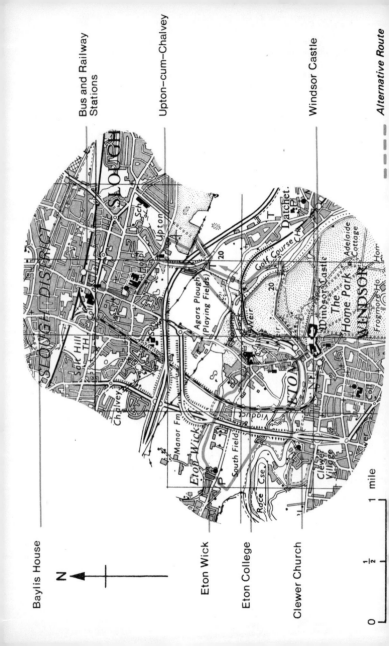

N

Baylis House

Eton Wick

Eton College

Clewer Church

Bus and Railway
Stations

Upton–cum–Chalvey

Windsor Castle

Alternative Route

0   ½   1 mile

arches. Keep along the side of the field (right) to go under the railway (opened in 1849). On the far side do not go ahead but turn right to go down a stone step into a field and turn left to continue westwards.

Walk along the field to go under the Windsor by-pass. Continue westwards along Eton Great Common. There are new houses to the left and a stream to the right.

On reaching an iron footbridge (right) bear half left towards the 'Greyhound' (a white building in the distance). Cross a stile to turn left along a metalled drive. At a junction turn right and then left by the 'Greyhound' to go along a road called The Walk and reach the main road at Eton Wick.

ETON WICK. The church of St. John Baptist was built in the late 1860s.

Cross the main road to find a gate just beyond the phone box. Follow the footpath ahead to reach a wide cross-track. Turn left on to the track which runs in a south-easterly direction towards Windsor Castle (see below). To the left of the Castle is the tower of Eton parish church and Eton College Chapel.

On approaching the tunnels under the by-pass, bear half right on to a narrow footpath to walk towards some trees. Do not turn down the sunken lane but keep ahead to the river. Walk across the wooden bridge and keep ahead for 400 yards to re-join the river opposite Clewer Church.

CLEWER. St. Andrew's is mostly Norman and William the Conqueror is said to have visited the building. Canon Thomas Carter, a leader of the Oxford Movement and rector from 1844 to 1880, was associated with the nearby House of Mercy in Hatch Lane where prostitutes, saved by Gladstone, were sent for rehabilitation.

Keep the water to the right and follow the bankside under the by-pass, over two bridges and under the railway. On reaching Eton leave the water to follow a path up the side of Eton College

Boat House to the 'Waterman's Arms'. Keep forward up Brocas
Street to join Eton High Street. Turn right to cross Windsor
Bridge.

WINDSOR BRIDGE was until recently the boundary between
Eton, Buckinghamshire and the Royal Borough of New Windsor
in the Royal County of Berkshire. The iron bridge, opened in 1823,
replaced a wooden structure and until 1898 a toll-gate stood on the
Windsor side.
     Ahead is Windsor.

WINDSOR. William the Conqueror built a fortress where the
Round Tower stands. The oldest parts of the present Castle date
from Henry II. Elizabeth I built the North Terrace from which
visitors can enjoy the view across Home Park and Eton. After
Charles II's reign the buildings fell into disrepair. George III was
the next monarch to live here and under his son, George IV, the
castle was transformed by Wyatville, who built the Waterloo
Chamber. Prince Albert died here in 1861. The Queen is often in
residence at weekends. The State Apartments are usually open
Mondays to Saturdays 10 30 to 17 00 (15 00 November to
March) and also summer Sundays 13 30 to 17 00 but closed
during Easter, Ascot week and most of December; admission 60p,
children 30p.
     St. George's Chapel was built just before the Reformation in
perpendicular style and has a magnificent vaulted roof. Those
buried in the chapel include Henry VI, Henry VIII, Jane Seymour,
Edward VI, Charles I, George III, George IV, William IV, Edward
VII, Queen Alexandra, George V and Queen Mary. Amongst the
banners of the Garter Knights are those of Sir Harold Wilson and
Lord Longford. St. George's Chapel is open in the early after-
noons, admission 80p, children and pensioners 40p.
     The town's Guildhall was completed by Christopher Wren and
the columns (which do not touch the ceiling) were added reluc-
tantly by Wren to confound the Council, who thought the building looked unsafe. In the 1860s J. S. Stone wrote the hymn *The*

Church's One Foundation whilst he was a curate at nearby All Saint's Church. The Naval tradition of pulling the gun carriage at Royal funerals began at Windsor & Eton Central Station during Queen Victoria's Funeral, when (owing to cold) the horses pulling the gun-carriage became restless and, at the whispered advice of Prince Louis (the late Lord Mountbatten's father), Edward VII allowed the Navy to take over.

At the cross-roads beneath the Castle the walk continues to the left to pass the George V Memorial (right) and the Windsor and Eton Riverside Station (left).

WINDSOR AND ETON RIVERSIDE STATION. The railway arrived here in 1849 after protracted negotiations over permission to cross Home Park. Eventually, the London & South-Western Railway paid £60,000 which was used to improve the Castle. Royal House, at the side, is the former Royal Waiting Room.

Continue past the Station (left) and just beyond Royal House bear left to leave the main road and follow a park road (where a sign points to 'Home Park Pavilions'). On reaching a car park (left) leave the road and go over to the far corner to cross the railway by a footbridge.

Turn right to walk along a lane which follows the Thames (left). Across the water there is a glimpse of Eton College Chapel. After a short distance the way leaves the river to run through a boatyard. Beyond the tower (left) go over to the river to walk through a small gate and follow the grass river bank. When the Thames bears southwards, cross a stile and go under the railway bridge. Continue ahead with the river.

On approaching a road bridge go up the grass bank and cross the river. Follow Windsor Road for a short distance. As the road bends go left through a gap and cross a footbridge to reach a golf course. Turn left to join a gravelled path. Where the firm path fades away keep forward on the grass. At the far end of the course go ahead up a narrow path and before the railway bridge bear half right at a fork to go under an arch.

Beyond the railway, follow an enclosed path to Pococks Lane. Cross the road and go right for a few yards to walk down a short enclosed path which leads to a field. Keep ahead along a stream (left) to cross a stile at the far end.

Turn right along the road (The Myrke) and go left (by a phone box) to cross Datchet Road. Follow the metalled lane which crosses the M4 Motorway to enter Upton Court Park. On the far side of the bridge leave the metalled lane and go left along the edge of the playing field. At the far end turn right up the second side of the field. Keep forward and on approaching a gateway in the second corner turn left (just before the gate) to cross a hidden stile. Bear right with the footpath which opens out and leads to another stile by a road. Cross the stile and turn left along the road to pass the entrance to Upton Court and Upton Church.

UPTON-CUM-CHALVEY. The Norman Church has a south aisle added by Benjamin Ferrey. Herschel (see page 1) is buried under the tower. Fordham, Queen Victoria's jockey, is buried in the churchyard (north side) in a tomb marked 'Tis the pace that kills'. Until the Reformation the church was under the monks of Merton Priory who built Upton Court, and later the home (in the 18th century) of Paul Nash's great great grandfather (see page 14). Many believe that this church, and not Stoke Poges (see page 15), inspired Gray's *Elegy in a Country Churchyard*. The 'Red Cow', on the north side of the roundabout, dates from the 16th century.

Keep ahead to retrace the outward route to the centre of Slough.

2 A Princess, an Artist and a Poet

UXBRIDGE – IVER – LANGLEY PARK – GEORGE GREEN – STOKE POGES – SLOUGH
$9\frac{1}{4}$ MILES

PRINCESS MARINA, Paul Nash and Thomas Gray all knew this area as home. Nash said it was 'real country, only 15 miles from London'. The lanes and fields remain untouched by expanding London and are now at the end of the Underground, only 40 minutes from Baker Street.

UXBRIDGE: Underground (Metropolitan and Piccadilly Lines). Bus 98, 128, 204, 207, 222, 224. Green Line 790.

IVER: London Country Bus 458, 484 (Sundays). Or British Rail.

GEORGE GREEN: London Country Bus 452, 457 (Mondays to Saturdays).

STOKE POGES: London Country Bus 353.

STOKEPLACE FARM: London Country Bus 353.

SLOUGH: Bus 81. Green Line Coach 701, 704, 726. Or British Rail.

UXBRIDGE was an important stop on the coaching route from London. The Market House, opposite the station, is 18th-century. St. Margaret's dates from the 14th century and has a fine hammer-beam roof. In 1645 there was an abortive peace negotiation at the 'Crown' inn between representatives of Charles I and his opponents in the Civil War. The new Hillingdon Civic Centre is at the south end of the High Street.

On leaving Uxbridge Underground Station go ahead along Windsor Street which runs at the side of the Market House and St. Margaret's. At a main road keep forward with the old burial ground to the left. Cross the second main road by the lofty pedestrian bridge. At the end of the ramp on the far side keep ahead for a few yards to turn right down Wellington Road.

At the far end of the road cross Fray's River and keep ahead on the metalled path across the playing field. On reaching a road continue forward and follow it round to the right to join Waterloo Road and meet Rockingham Road at the 'Dolphin'.

Turn left along Rockingham Road to cross the canal and pass the 'General Eliott' (left) and the 'Pipemaker Arms' (right). On reaching St. John's Church (left) turn left to walk through the churchyard and cross a stream. Go right along Culvert Lane to cross Cowley Mill Road (by the 'Sportsman's Hall') and enter Longbridge Way.

Keep forward when the tarmac ends to go through a gate and follow an enclosed path to the River Colne. Bear left with the river and follow the narrow footpath which runs near the water (right), but sometimes through thick undergrowth, for ¾ mile. On the way the footpath crosses a private access road and, just before a footbridge, a stile. Do not cross the footbridge but keep ahead to reach Iver Lane (at the Cape Boards building).

Turn right to cross the bridge and follow Iver Lane into Buckinghamshire. After 300 yards go right up a rough lane (just before a bus stop).

The way bears westwards and has various surfaces. At Daffodil Cottage the lane narrows and after a double bend meets a white gate. Keep ahead over the stile at the side of the gate. At a second double bend the way crosses Colne Brook.

Continue forward past a row of converted buildings. The footpath narrows and bears slightly leftwards along the top of Delaford

Manor's garden. At a gateway go over the wooden stile and follow the narrowing path which runs gently uphill and bears slightly right. On meeting a whitewashed cottage at Coppins Farm the track becomes the metalled Coppins Lane. There is a glimpse of Coppins (right) before the lane meets Bangors Road South. To the left there is the village of Iver.

IVER. The partly Norman church has a trace of the original Saxon building and a late 17th-century font. The 'Swan' inn is 16th-century. Iver Station is ¾ mile to the south.

The walk continues to the right to pass the main entrance to Coppins.

COPPINS. In the Middle Ages the original house was the home of Copyns. The present building is 19th-century and was occupied by John Mitchell who arranged Queen Victoria's theatre outings. Later it became the home of her grand-daughter, Princess Victoria, and on her death in 1935 it passed to the Duke of Kent who had just married Princess Marina. He filled the house with antiques and his large collection of clocks. Every week flowers and vegetables were sent to their Belgrave Square house. The Queen, Prince Philip and Princess Margaret came here as children and other visitors included Queen Mary, Mrs. Simpson (later Duchess of Windsor), Princess Juliana (Queen of the Netherlands), Churchill and General Smuts. Princess Marina continued to live here after her husband's death in 1942 and only moved out in 1961 when her son, the present Duke of Kent, married. He sold the house in 1972 and a new owner pulled down part of the wall to give a clear view of the building.

Continue along the road and after 300 yards turn left by White Cottage to walk down Love Green Lane. On reaching a garage (left) go half right (through iron railings) across a small triangle of grass and over a driveway to a road. Go right for a few yards to cross a wooden stile on the left by a wooden gate. Go ahead to follow a hedge (right). Keep forward beyond a disused iron swing

gate to cross a stile on the far side of the field. Follow the hedge (left) which soon gives way to a view of Heath Lodge. Beyond a stile ahead is Wood Lane. Iver Heath and Wood Lane House are $\frac{1}{4}$ mile to the right.

WOOD LANE. Paul Nash, aged 12, came to live at Wood Lane House in 1901 when it was built for the family. He attended St. Margaret's, Iver Heath where his father was churchwarden. For a time he travelled into London each evening for commercial art training. Cycling back from Uxbridge Station at night he was often moved by the shapes and shadows he observed. At the house he worked on *Nude, Iver Heath* (his wife in the garden), *Landscape at Wood Lane, Tree Group Iver Heath, Window of the Morning Room* and *Bird Garden* (now in the National Museum of Wales, Cardiff) which shows part of the garden in 1911. Ben Nicholson stayed at Wood Lane House when Nash was concentrating on landscape drawing. A local resident gave him an introduction to Sir William Richmond who helped Nash to stage his first exhibition in 1912. The house was sold in 1929 when Paul's father died. Paul Nash became one of the major British painters of his generation. He also designed book-jackets, bindings, furnishing textiles, rugs, stage sets, ceramics, glassware, posters and even Tilly Losch's bathroom. His work for London Transport included moquette upholstery and several posters. War paintings by Paul and his brother John can be seen in the Imperial War Museum. Until recently Fernleigh, the 19th-century white house (at the north end), was the home of Tom Stoppard who wrote many of his plays in the large study.

The walk continues down Bellswood Lane opposite. After just over $\frac{1}{4}$ mile the road meets Billet Lane. Cross the road and walk up the fenced footpath by the entrance to Treal Farm. At the far end go through the wooden gate ahead to enter Langley Park. Follow the rough drive. There is a glimpse of the mansion (see below) and after $\frac{1}{4}$ mile another drive joins from the right.

Keep forward and go right by the stables (where the way becomes metalled) to cross the main drive.

LANGLEY PARK was once a Royal Park which Charles I granted to Sir John Kederminster who founded the chain library in Langley Church. The third Duke of Marlborough had the present house built in the 1740s as he wanted a country home nearer to London than Blenheim Palace. Langley Park now forms just one section of the Colne Valley Park which stretches from Rickmansworth to Staines.

Cross the main drive to take a rough path (ignore the 'permit only' notice) which soon bends to the left and meets a pair of iron gates. Go through the swing gates at the side and follow the path which gently bears right across the park to another gateway. Walk through the swing gates to pass two houses and a lodge (left) by a gateway.

Keep ahead up George Green Road to the main road at George Green. On the left is the entrance to Westmoor House.

WESTMOOR HOUSE dates from 1664 and was until recently the Langley Marish Rectory. William Nash (Paul Nash's great-great-grandfather) of Upton Court (see page 8) bought the Rectory for his son, William, who as owner of the estate received the tithes and became 'lay rector' with the parish work undertaken by a 'perpetual curate' who was known as the 'vicar'. Although William became a non-conformist he remained 'rector' and the post eventually passed to John Nash (Paul's grandfather). As a child in the 1890s Paul often stayed here, enjoying the ride from the station, tea under the mulberry tree, shooting parties and Christmas gatherings. There were numerous visitors and earlier his grandfather had offered Disraeli refreshment here. Paul particularly liked riding to Langley Church with his grandfather as the local people waved and curtseyed. Paul recalled that the 'inside of the church was so enthralling that it was difficult to keep up an appearance of interest in the service'. Paul Nash and his wife are buried in the churchyard (at the side of the walled Harvey grave). His grand-father died in 1900 and the family sold the house in 1907 when Paul was living in Wood Lane (see page 13).

The walk continues opposite at the side of the 'Double Century'. (There is a footbridge over the dual carriageway near the 'George' to the left). Climb over the stile and walk ahead to cross a second stile and a field. The 'Double Century' is to the right. Go over the stile and follow a wire fence (left) to go over a further stile. Bear half left across the field (or left round the edge) to find a wooden stile by an iron gate on the far side. Beyond the stile bear quarter right across the next field to cross a stile by a tree. Keep ahead up the side of a field to cross a stile by a gateway at Deadman's Lane.

Turn left along the road and just around the bend go right on to a narrow path which runs through the belt of trees to a stile. Bear half left across the large field to find a stile in the far corner. Go ahead at the T-junction of rough lanes to pass Bell Farm Livery Stable (right) where the way becomes metalled. After $\frac{1}{3}$ mile the lane meets a main road. Turn left and before the entrance to Wexham Park Hospital go right over a stile. Walk ahead across a field to cross another stile. Keep ahead by the hedge (left) to cross a third stile. Bear half right up the field to go over a stile by a white gate and join a lane at a bend. Go left up the wide stony way to reach a main road.

Turn right and then left to walk along Duffield Park. At the far end go ahead over the grass to go through a swing gate. Follow the enclosed path over a drive through another swing gate to cross 3 more drives before reaching a swing gate at the end of the path. To the right, across the road, is Gray's Field, Stoke Poges.

STOKE POGES. 'Stoke' means 'stockaded place' and 'Poges' comes from Robert Poges who was the manor's tenant from 1290 to 1330. Sir Edward Coke, the jurist, entertained Elizabeth I at the house. Charles I was held prisoner there for 12 days in August 1647. Thomas Penn, son of Pennsylvania's founder, bought the estate in 1760. The house is the setting for Thomas Gray's poem *A Long Story* which features Mrs. Tyack and Mr. Groom who are buried in the south-west corner of the churchyard. Gray used to stay with his mother and aunt at nearby Stoke Court and between 1745 and 1750 wrote his *Elegy in a Country Churchyard* at their home and under the yew tree (behind the kiosk) opposite the church porch. The tower was once the poem's 'ivy-mantled tow'r' (see also page 8). Gray is buried outside the church opposite the east window of the 16th-century Hastings Chapel. The scene has hardly changed since Henrik Frans de Cort exhibited his painting of the tomb at the Royal Academy in 1797. The monument in the nearby field was designed by Wyatt and erected by Penn's grandson in 1799. The 250-year-old elms, mentioned in the Elegy, have recently had to be cut down.

The walk continues to the left along an enclosed footpath which crosses a road after 300 yards. Keep ahead up the side (right) of a field. At the far end continue forward between two unfenced fields to reach a rough tree-lined lane known as Muddy Lane. Turn left along the lane to meet a main road by Stokeplace Farm where there is a bus stop. Go right to walk into Slough. The road leads directly to the bus and railway stations.

SLOUGH: See page 1.

3 Top of Dizzyland

TODAY we explore the soft Chiltern woods lining the slopes of the Hughenden Valley with remote and beautiful prospects that so delighted Disraeli, the great Victorian statesman who built his home nearby. Some straggling settlements, hard to avoid, bring the tour to the gentle slopes overlooking the next great fold of the Chilterns watered by the uncertain waters of the River Misbourne. A great day out in the country.

GREAT MISSENDEN: Underground (Metropolitan Line) to Amersham, then cross-platform interchange or British Rail direct to Great Missenden.

WIDMER END: London Country Bus 364.

AMERSHAM: Underground (Metropolitan Line).

GREAT MISSENDEN. In the courtyard of the inn where you leave the High Street (see below) is a long half-timbered building once used as a courthouse. The Manor Court of Great Missenden sat there to decide local affairs. The 'Crown' marks the site of an earlier inn, first built in 1843. Missenden is a wonderfully lively village that has learnt to live with the motor age.

From Great Missenden station turn downhill and go right, along the village street until you reach the 'George and Dragon' (there was no name on the inn when the survey was carried out but a clear signboard). Take the tiny passageway alongside the inn, then bear left and right to Twichell Street and so under the railway to a rough gravel track where you go right, then left almost at once by a fine field path towards distant Angling Spring Wood.

Inside the shade of the beeches, strike left at once, climbing the uncertain ground to a trackway that at the top winds half left to another cross-track after only a few yards. Turn right past the house; this is a pretty hedge-enclosed way that wanders in woodland for about 300 yards until it sweeps sharply left. Leave it at the bend to cross a gateside stile on the right, and trace out the clear woodland path as it travels just inside the wood to a stile at a field. Cross and go straight on to the lane at the houses opposite.

Now go along Church Path, the wide track opposite you and a little to your right. This passes houses to plunge into another wonderful wood (Nairdwood). Again, using the border path, carry on for some 350 yards until you reach a clear path joining from the left as the wood thins to allow a field either side. Go left along this new path – also a border track that keeps inside the tree cover, but near to the right-hand edge of the wood.

After a ¼ mile you look for a path on your *right* that will leave the wood; it is a good idea to keep as close to the side of the tree-line as a path will allow. You will see this exit path leading out towards a small gate, but this is deceptive as upon reaching it, you will find the public path starts to its right, and goes clearly forward, with a hedge left, to the main Prestwood road at the 'Polecat' inn. (If you have missed the path from the wood and found that you have reached a road, don't worry; just turn right along the road, and right again to the 'Polecat'.)

A footpath sign in the inn yard shows where the next stile is – at the end of the car park. Cross the stile into a small field and keep near its right side to cross another stile into a wide meadow. The view from here reaches towards the Upper Hughenden Valley; you will agree a splendid prospect. The way is downhill, half leftwards over the grass, to a corner stile in its bottom left corner.

On reaching the little curving lane, go uphill for 150 yards to enter Longfield Wood by a wide gate, right, which is signposted. Keep to the rutted track as it climbs steeply between the trees to

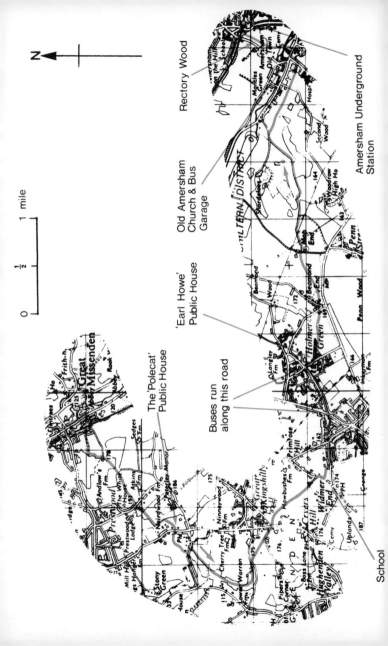

N

0   ½   1 mile

Great Missenden

Rectory Wood

Old Amersham Church & Bus Garage

'Earl Howe' Public House

The 'Polecat' Public House

Buses run along this road

School

Amersham Underground Station

reach high but level ground. Now simply follow the woodland track, remembering always to keep as level as you can and avoid dropping away to the right.

You will pass a pylon in a tiny clearing, then the nature of the wood changes a little, the trees becoming less close, allowing more ground growth to interfere with your path. In another 200 yards or so you will find the main path does fall a little, before starting to run on, hugging the top (left-hand) side of the wood and presenting some rather nasty ancient holes to walk around (obviously where great trees have tumbled). When the way turns leftward, the track gets clearer and very broad. This is one of the most pleasant parts of this wood, about a mile in length. You will emerge at a small lane where you take the signposted path on the opposite side, and some 50 yards downhill.

Go forward towards a small remnant of hedge and keep uphill, with the bushes on your right. When surveyed, an ancient stile remained on the skyline to confirm the direction of your path, but keep a straight course, with silos away to the left, until you cross a track by stiles. Finally, with a hedgeline on your right, you will reach a stile by an iron gate at a lane (opposite 'Piper's Crow'). Go left to the main road and cross to a signposted stile opposite – just to the right of a road.

Now a bold field track sweeps ahead through the centre of a field to pass through a wide gap into a second meadow. Keep forward to a large cultivated field, where the path takes its left side to run down to another stile at a lane. This runs forward to reach a broad road at Widmer End.

Go uphill to take the first turning left, an estate road leading to Widmer Schools. Then go by footpath around the school grounds to a main road, turn downhill for 500 yards until the turn at the bottom of the slope, then carry straight ahead by a signposted narrow footpath that climbs up between gardens to a main road which you cross.

Go straight opposite by the straight road ahead. Although served by buses, this ½ mile is hard to avoid, but look out for Earl Howe road on the right, at a junction by a pond. Turn along this road, soon passing the 'Earl Howe' inn, and take the next left turning (Hoggs Lane). After some settlements the fieldpath resumes, leading straight forward to Beaumont End (the farm and lane ahead). Go over the stiles ahead and over another little lane almost at once, and continue ahead by a rough wide signposted track (passing a motor works on the left). This leads over another track at a lodge, and runs, by stiles, over two more fields to Mop End, another lonely little hamlet.

Once again cross the lane directly to a signposted track that wanders on through firs before hurrying you round a corner to reveal a pylon. The track turns and twists until you stand, at stiles, overlooking the upper pastures of the Shardeloes estate. Keep to the right of the long, sloping meadow which shows the far side of the Misbourne Valley.

Go through an iron kissing-gate, near a recently constructed mansion in the Georgian style, to the drive, but take in directly through a second kissing-gate on the right. Now go half left over a large field until the path joins the boundary path at trees. Now go right all the way until it reaches the Wycombe road near some over-improved cottages at Amersham. To the left is the Broad-way, Town Hall and the Church, where you can catch your bus.

AMERSHAM. St. Mary's dates from the 13th century and has, in the Drake Chapel, some 15th-century brasses and monuments. King John granted an annual fair which is held, during the church's patronal festival (19 and 20 September) in the main street. The Market Hall was built by Sir William Drake in 1682. Near Station Road, in the corner of a field, there is a memorial to local Lollards who were burnt at the stake. Cromwell dined at the 'Griffin' in 1645. Bury Farm was the home of William Penn's first wife.

Opposite the bus garage an early 19th-century notice warns against 'ballad singers and other vagrants'.

There is a pleasant path to the station that starts on the far side of the church; reach it by the clear path through the churchyard.

After turning left for a few yards, the metalled path climbs up to Rectory Wood. On the far side of the wood turn right to the main road and railway bridge. The station is reached by turning right on the far side of the bridge.

4 Chesham Switchback

CHESHAM – ASHLEY GREEN – JASON HILL – CHESHAM
11½ MILES

THIS IS an exhilarating day out amid the Chiltern ridges and 'bottoms' – a relaxing rough-and-tumble through beechwoods, farms and along wide grassy slopes where the countryside fuses into a pattern of fields below.

Remember that farm workers take care to be well-shod, and as farm surrounds can be poached up by animals, it is wise to follow the example of the countryman.

CHESHAM: Underground (Metropolitan Line).

ASHLEY GREEN: London Country Bus 353.

LEY HILL: London Country Bus 336 (Mondays to Saturdays).

CHESHAM is mentioned in Domesday Book; it probably gave its name to the pleasant river on which it stands. Chesham has long been known for its local timber products, but is now turning into a large commuter dormitory society as new housing continues to extend up its steep hillsides.

Turn left outside Chesham Station to the High Street, and reach Lowdnes Park by the short road starting from the roundabout ahead. You must cross forward over a second roundabout, before you can turn left, passing some pleasant ornamental gardens, to the Town Church. Follow the path on the right to a building; transfer to a clear grassy path only a yard or so to the left with the tree-line on your immediate left. From a gap in the upper left corner of the field, the path runs down to two stiles, which you cross to reach a field from which comes the first broad panoramic view over the Chiltern folds towards Hundridge and Missenden.

Avoid a path running downwards, and walk along the upper slope of the field, keeping close to the trees now on your right. Carry on through two large fields and you reach a kissing-gate and an enclosed path that runs by the back gardens of houses before winding right to reach the main road (Chartridge Lane). Here you turn left. The road winds right and then left. As it turns leftwards, and just after you cross Berkeley Avenue (a side road on the right), you will see a post box. As you pass the box bear off over the wide grass verge on the right and on to a small enclosed footpath that passes the backs of gardens before turning left towards a field. Go under the bar stile now and down the slope towards a lane at Portobello Farm, the group of buildings near the far field corner. Now turn left.

Five hundred yards along this pretty lane you will see a footpath sign (marked for Mount Nugent) by a gate on the right. (The buildings of Hazeldean Farm can be seen on the lower slopes of the hill.) Cross the gate and follow the good concrete track leading towards the farm buildings, but keep forward, as it turns, to use a field-path running the side of a field to a stile at a beechwood. Now you must pick your way upwards (paths in woods are often elusive) to a track that runs along the top edge of the wood. Follow this track only a short way to the left (you will soon see Mount Nugent Farm in the field on your right) until you reach a stile on the right. Leave the wood now, cross the stile, and go over grass to a gate-side stile, passing the farm buildings on your immediate right. Carry on by the farm track to a road.

The next path starts directly opposite; after a few yards it turns sharp left to run beside the back gardens of houses, with a field on your right. After passing into a second field, turn right, and trace out a field-path that runs never far from the hedgeline on the right.

At the far end of the field the path makes a left turn for 50 yards or so to pass around a projecting spur of a wood; it then curves right and plunges between the trees. Later the path winds right to reach a stile at a field; when you cross the stile you are overlooking a sheltered little vale.

Go downhill now, keeping close to the trees on the left to cross a wooden stile in the lower hedge about 25 yards from the corner of the field. Turn right along the clear path that runs along the length of the field beside the hedge. After passing through iron gates, you emerge on a road at Chesham Vale.

Now turn left to the 'Black Horse', a pleasant little rural inn. Leave the valley by the hedged cart-track opposite the 'Black Horse'. After passing a few settlements, the stony track runs uphill gently between tall hedges with the fields stretching upwards on either side. In $\frac{1}{4}$ mile, at a side track, the flinty track you are on turns boldly right and continues its climb, now between trees, until you reach a height of over 525 feet, and there is open land ahead. Do *not* go into the field, however, but make a sharp left turn with the track just before the field.

The path, which now runs over the lines of an ancient rutted overgrown track, later winds around to Flampstead Farm. Turn right, over the gate and through the main yard, keeping on by the service road to the main Chesham Road near Ashley Green. Turn

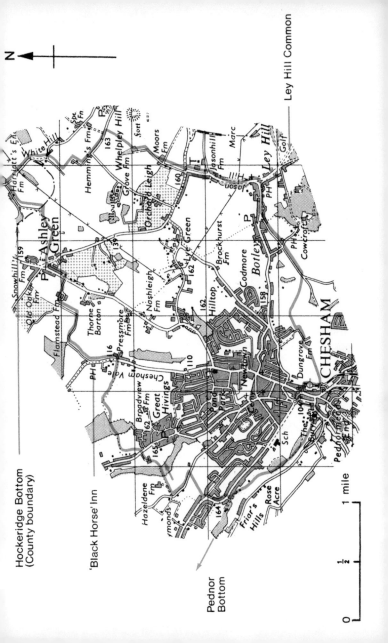

N

Hockeridge Bottom
(County boundary)

'Black Horse' Inn

Pednor
Bottom

Ley Hill Common

0   ½   1 mile

CHESHAM

Ashley Green
Whelpley Hill
White Hill
Harriatt's End
Ley Hill
Orchard Leigh
Lye Green
Botley
Brockhurst Fm
Hilltop
Codmore
Dungrove
Newtown
Great Hivings
Broadview Fm
Chesham Vale
Pressmore Fm
Thorne Barton
Flamstead Fm
Old Oaks Fm
Snowhill Fm
Hemming's Fm
Grove Fm
Moors Fm
Masonhill Fm
Cowcroft
Nashleigh Fm
Hazeldene Fm
Friar's Hills
Rose Acre
Pednormead End
The Park
159
163
160
162
158
162
116
110
162
164

left for 200 yards or so to the church marking the green and crossroads.

ASHLEY GREEN. Many of the houses are sheltered from the main road traffic by the wide belt of grass that gives this settlement its name. The church is modern.

Leave Ashley Green by a track beside the village school almost opposite the church. After crossing two stout modern stiles that mark the course of the footpath past a very hazardous enclosure, keep near the left hedge and continue gently downhill to a gate and onwards by the broad walk towards the valley of Hockeridge Bottom.

This is a very open part of London's countryside, with hardly a rooftop to be seen. It is the border country between Hertfordshire and Buckinghamshire. The field-track reaches lower ground at a field corner and swerves leftwards uphill to run beside a small wood to take you between the well-kept buildings of Harriotsend Farm and so down to a tiny sunken lane which later affords another look at Hockeridge Bottom as it runs, right, to White Hill.

When the lane bears left near at the top of a sharp rise, carry on ahead by a track that enters a belt of trees. The track later makes a left turn and runs up to the Sale's Farm. Here it passes the farm (on the right) and makes a right-angled turn at the last bars (avoid the field-path running ahead). Keep the farm still on your immediate right until a hard track is reached. Follow this round to a lane and keep on, along the broad greensward to the right of the tarmac for 400 yards until you reach a signposted footpath on the right, opposite a track. Go forward over grass, beside strands of wire, until the path enters a wood. On the far side, bear left around the side of a large field to a rough track that runs, with a hedge still on your left, around another side of the field to Moor's Farm, the buildings ahead.

Walk on through the farmyard and continue ahead to a road,

which you cross and continue ahead along Jason Hill, opposite. This road runs into a shallow valley on its way to Leyhill Common – just as it nears the lower ground, transfer to a pleasant footpath that runs parallel to the road, but through a screen of bushes and trees a few yards to its right.

LEY HILL. Originally just a hamlet near Latimer, the village has grown by its closeness to Chesham. An attractive common, which provides a golf course, makes the village rather scattered.

Rejoin the road at the approach to the Ley Hill cross-roads and bear right for $\frac{1}{4}$ mile to Broomstick Lane, on the left side of the road. After passing a house or two, the lane becomes a pleasant country track.

Carry on over a crossing track to the rough flint track opposite (Trapp's Lane), and continue downhill for another 250 yards or so until trees appear ahead and the track widens at a signposted footpath crossing (when surveyed the signs were vandalized). Leave the trackway here and cross over a gate into the field on the right, and go half-left over steeply rising grassland to cross a pair of stiles. Keeping this same direction, continue over a second meadow, gradually leaving the hedgeline on the right) and follow the path that later takes you past school playing fields and a house or two to another broad track, with Dungrove Farm buildings ahead, and slightly left.

Go over the stiles and on by the grassy path to the farm. It tends to be a little muddy here, but turn right at the farm perimeter on to a deeply rutted track which soon bears left around the field. When it ends at a field on your right, the way is clear for the final run down to Chesham.

Go half left over grass all the way down the slope, crossing stiles, until the way narrows to a steeply-falling path between bushes. On lower ground, follow the path left, then right, to cross the Metropolitan Line by a bridge and then right again to the station.

5 The Pope, The President and Ovaltine

ST. ALBANS – BEDMOND – ABBOTS LANGLEY – KING'S LANGLEY –
WATFORD
10½ MILES

THIS WALK crosses the Ovaltine Farm which encompasses a stretch of countryside known to Nicholas Breakspear, the only English Pope, and President Carter's ancestors.

ST. ALBANS: Underground to High Barnet then bus 84. Green Line 707, 717, 724, 727.

BEDMOND: Green Line 719. London Country bus 347, 348 (Mondays to Saturdays).

ABBOTS LANGLEY: Green Line 719. London Country bus W4, 347, 348 (Mondays to Saturdays).

KINGS LANGLEY: Green Line 708, 719. London Country bus 301 (Mondays to Saturdays), 302 (Mondays to Saturdays), 322. Or British Rail.

WATFORD: Underground (Metropolitan Line). Bus 142, 258 (Mondays to Saturdays). Green Line 708, 719, 724, 727.

ST. ALBANS. In 209 the Roman soldier Albanus was led out of Verulamium (see page 30) and executed for refusing to renounce Christianity. Later an abbey (now the cathedral) was built on the execution site and the tomb of St. Alban, the first English martyr, became an object of pilgrimage. Roman tiles were used by the

Normans to build the tower. The watching chamber by the Saint's tomb is 14th century. Opposite is the tomb of Henry IV's son. Humphrey, Duke of Gloucester. Nicholas Breakspear, who was to become Pope Adrian IV, attended the Abbey School but was refused admission to the Benedictine Order. He entered a French monastery and, having become a cardinal, visited the St. Albans community. When Breakspear was elected to the Papacy in 1154, the abbot took gifts to Rome and was allowed to wear a mitre. Adrian's widowed father became a monk here and is now buried in the sanctuary. The 14th-century gateway was besieged by John Ball and his followers during the Peasants' Revolt in 1381. One of the last abbots was the non-resident Cardinal Wolsey. St. Alban's shrine was destroyed at the Dissolution – although much of the smashed pedestal has been pieced together again. The church was retained for the parish and became a cathedral in 1877 when a new Anglican diocese was created. The face of the new Archbishop of Canterbury has joined the gargoyles on the south side. Before the Reformation candles were sold to pilgrims at Waxhouse Gate. Opposite there is the 13th-century Clock Tower which houses the curfew bell (open summer weekends 10 30 to 17 00, admission 10p, children 5p). One of the Eleanor Crosses used to stand nearby. French Row was occupied by French troops in 1216. The 'Fleur de Lys', said to have been built by a 15th-century Abbey sub-cellarer, stands on the site of a house where King John of France was held after the Battle of Poitiers. Two battles were fought in St. Peter's Street during the Wars of the Roses.

Go through the Abbey gateway (beyond the Cathedral's west end) to walk down Abbey Mill Lane – St. Alban walked up this road to his execution. Keep right where the lane divides. The 'Fighting Cocks' is on the left.

YE OLD FIGHTING COCKS is said to have been a medieval pigeon house and fishing lodge. The building was part of the monastery until the Reformation when it became an inn. For a time it was a centre of cockfighting. The pub is claimed to be the oldest inhabited licensed house in the country, but in late years has suffered extensive 'improvement'.

Cross the river Ver and follow the path ahead with a lake to the right. Soon the way passes the site of the London Gate to the Roman town of Verulamium. Watling Street ran from the left into the town on the right.

VERULAMIUM. Roman armies occupied this site in AD43. The hypocaust (in the middle of the park) and the Verulamium Museum (at St. Michael's on the far side of the park) are open daily 10 00 (14 00 Sundays) to 17 00 (17 30 Sundays, or 16 00 in winter), admission 25p children 10p (ticket admits to both). Just beyond the museum is the Roman Theatre open 10 00 to dusk, admission 25p, students 10p and children 8p.

Continue forward below the Roman Wall (right) to reach a road beyond a footbridge. Take the footpath ahead which runs between a playing field and new houses (right). The path crosses three roads. Where the houses end bear left on to a rough path and after a few yards turn right, through a gap in the fence, to follow a path up a sloping field.

On reaching a wood go left and, when the trees end, right to cross a motorway. Keep ahead over the stile and follow Park Wood (right) to reach a lane. Go right along the lane for 200 yards and turn left into Furzebushes Lane. This road bears left to a sharp right turn. Do not go right, but keep forward to enter a field and turn half right to climb up to a lane by the National Rose Society.

ROYAL NATIONAL ROSE SOCIETY was founded in 1876 and exists to extend the knowledge of and love for the rose. Here there are 30,000 plants consisting of over 1,650 different varieties and species. Open 14 June to 30 September (except 25 August) 09 00 to 17 00 (Sundays 14 00 to 18 00): admission 60p, children free.

Go to the right along the lane and, at the end of the Rose

Society's ground, turn left to find a footpath. When the garden (left) ends keep ahead to a wooden stile on the far side. Keep forward across a further field. At a fence, ahead, stay to the right of the drinking trough to follow a track running down to Noke Farm. Turn right before the new farm buildings to find a wooden stile leading to a lane.

Turn right along the road for 100 yards to go left up the private road to Holt Farm. Follow the rough road past the farmhouse and a barn (left) to bear ½ right towards a wood. (Local walkers usually continue to the T-junction and turn right). The way soon joins the side of a motorway and runs up to Blunt's Lane.

Go left across the bridge and, after a short distance, turn left down Millhouse Lane – a metalled road which narrows and becomes rough after Searches Farm. Ignore all turnings and follow the lane, which becomes metalled again by Millhouse Farm (left), to reach Bedmond.

BEDMOND. Pope Adrian IV, the only English Pope, was born here about 1100 at Breakspeare Farm which was demolished in the early 1960s. As a cardinal he is believed to have visited his old home in about 1150 – four years before his election to the Papacy.

Go left along the High Street to pass the 'Bell' (left) and East Lane. (Breakspeare Farm was to the right where the new houses now stand). Continue ahead downhill to pass a cottage (right) and a bus stop. Go right up Sheppey's Lane. Ignore turnings to the left and right. At the end of the field to the left go over a stile to follow an enclosed path across the Ovaltine Farm. After just over a quarter of a mile the path crosses (at stiles) the main farm drive.

OVALTINE DAIRY FARM. The model farm, known as Parsonage Farm, was built in 1935 to produce milk needed for the manufacture of Ovaltine (see below). The Sussex farmhouse style buildings have been used in advertisements.

Keep ahead and at a T-junction turn right to walk along the side

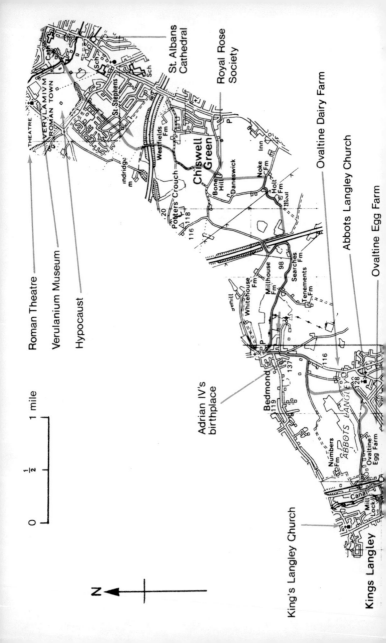

N

0   ½   1 mile

Roman Theatre

Verulamium Museum

Hypocaust

St. Albans Cathedral

Royal Rose Society

Ovaltine Dairy Farm

Abbots Langley Church

Ovaltine Egg Farm

Adrian IV's birthplace

King's Langley Church

Kings Langley

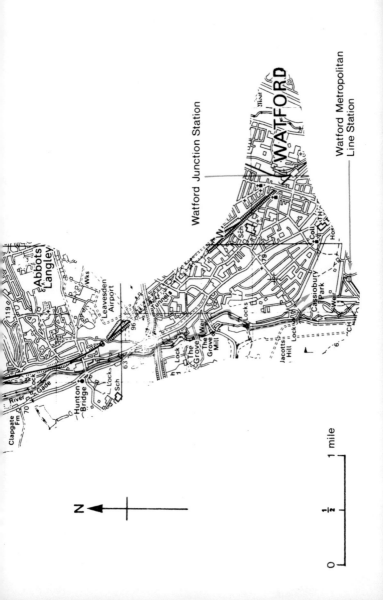

N

Watford

WATFORD

Watford Junction Station

Watford Metropolitan
Line Station

Abbots
Langley

Leavesden
Airport

Clapgate
Fm

River Gade

Hunton
Bridge

Locks

Sch

Lock

The
Grove

The
Grove
Mill

Locks

Tunnel

Cassiobury
Park

Weir

Jacotts
Hill

Lock

Locks

Sch

Sch

Coll

TH

Hos

0   ½   1 mile

of Abbots Langley village. After a few years there is a path on the
left which leads to the church.

ABBOTS LANGLEY. St. Lawrence's Church was built when
Pope Adrian was a child. He possibly saw the completed building
when he returned, as a cardinal, to Bedmond. His village friends
sent gifts to Rome when Nicholas was elected to the Papacy and in
1159, on hearing of his sudden death, they attended a requiem mass
in the church. He is buried in St. Peter's Rome but a plaque on
the south wall of the church here records his association with the
parish. Langley House, behind St. Saviour's Church, is now the
Salvatorian Father's Breakspear College.

The walk continues ahead and where the path enters a field,
beyond wooden barriers, keep forward and turn right at the end
of the field to reach a stile, by a gate, in the far corner. Turn left on
to the main drive which runs gently downhill. Beyond Woodside
Cottage (left) there is a view of King's Langley (see below) and the
Ovaltine factory.

OVALTINE FACTORY. Ovaltine was launched in 1865 by a
Swiss doctor, George Wander, who was investigating the nutri-
tional values of barley malt. This building was begun in 1913 and
the company then had its own barges to bring coal from Coventry
– a 10 to 14-day return journey. Today more than half the Ovaltine
produced here is exported. The drink, which has been the official
beverage at the Olympic Games, was taken up Everest by Sir
Edmund Hillary and Chris Bonnington, and around the world by
Sir Alec Rose.

Continue ahead to pass the entrance to the former Ovaltine Egg
Farm (left) where the way bears right and then left under the
railway. The path meets a main road at King's Langley.

KING'S LANGLEY. President Carter is descended from William
Le Carter who helped to rebuild the royal palace here in 1369 for
Edward III – a remaining wall can still be seen at the top of Langley

hill. Edward's son, Edmund of Langley (the first Duke of York)
was born here. On his death he was buried with his wife, Isabel of
Castile, in the Friary (now part of the New School) and at the
Dissolution the tomb was transferred to the parish church. In 1877
the tomb (which may have been intended for Richard III) was
moved from the chancel to the north chapel. Also in the chapel
(under a red velvet mat) is a brass to John Carter who lived at
nearby Jeffries Farm in the 16th century. The Reverend Edmund
Carter was vicar here in the 17th century. Richard III was first
buried at the Friary and moved to Westminster Abbey 10 years
later. Two scenes from Shakespeare's *Richard III* are set in King's
Langley.

Turn left and go south for 300 yards. Just beyond a refreshment
hut (and before the station) turn down a path on the right. Beyond
a stream the path meets the Grand Union Canal. Cross the bridge.

*To reach the centre of King's Langley go ahead and turn right at the
road.*

The walk continues by the canal. Go right to reach the water and
walk south (with the canal on the left).

After a lock there is a view of the Victorian Church at Hunton
Bridge. The waterside path runs under a bridge and beyond two
locks the way bends under a road. Just before a motorway the path
leaves the water for a short distance. After another lock the path
crosses the water and, beyond a bend, runs under the drive to The
Grove, an 18th-century mansion designed by Sir Robert Taylor.

At an S-bend the canal passes Grovemill House and then flows
under a road. Soon the path switches back to the west bank before
two locks. After nearly half a mile cross Bridge 167 just beyond
another lock and enter Cassiobury Park.

CASSIOBURY PARK. The home of the Earls of Essex was
pulled down in 1927 but the grounds remain as a park. Little

Cassiobury, next to Watford College and occupied by the Education Committee, was the dower-house.

After crossing a stream, just inside the park, bear right (but keep ahead for the centre of Watford). Beyond the model railway the path joins a stream. Near a footbridge (right) bear half left to follow a road out of the park. On reaching a residential area go left up Cassiobury Park Avenue. Just beyond Swiss Avenue (right) there is Watford Underground Station (Metropolitan Line).

WATFORD. Wata, a Saxon chief, settled here and from the 8th century until the Reformation the area belonged to St. Albans Abbey. The town became a stage coach stop and later expanded when the canal and railway were built. St. Mary's Church dates from the 13th century and the Morrison monuments are among Nicholas Stone's best work. Near the church is the Mrs. Elizabeth Fuller School which was built in 1704. At the south end of the High Street, behind the 18th-century house of Joseph Benskin, were the Victorian premises of Benskin's Brewery. At the side of the 'Joseph Benskin', on the corner of Market Street, there is a 15th-century window from a rest house which stood on the site. The town's oldest pub is the 16th-century 'One Crown' in the High Street.

6 Three Hertfordshire Houses

SALISBURY HALL – LONDON COLNEY – TYTTENHANGER PARK –
COLNEY HEATH – NORTH MYMMS – SALISBURY HALL
5, 6½ or 8¾ Miles

THIS IS a circular walk which passes across the grounds of three historic mansions. A red bus route, crossed three times, enables you to shorten the walk. The tour starts, for convenience, at Salisbury Hall, a few miles from St. Albans.

SALISBURY HALL: Bus 84 from High Barnet Underground station, or St. Albans. London Country Bus 313.

LONDON COLNEY: Bus 84. London Country Bus 313. Green Line 707, 717.

COLNEY HEATH: London Country Bus 342 (Mondays to Saturdays), 343.

WAGGON AND HORSES: Bus 84. London Country Bus 313.

SALISBURY HALL: The moated 17th-century manor house is the third on the site since the original was erected by the Saxons. In 1471 the Earl of Warwick and Salisbury set out from here to meet his death at the Battle of Barnet. There are traces of Tudor work which recall the residence of Sir John Cutler, Henry VIII's Treasurer. Charles II and Nell Gwynne were regular visitors and knew the house as it is now. It is said to be here that the king called up from the garden 'God Save the Earl of Burford' when Nell threatened to throw her baby from the window unless provision was made for him. The present Duke of St. Albans is the baby's descendant. The house was the home, for some years, of

Churchill's mother who was often visited by Winston. In the 1930s Sir Nigel Gresley designed Pacific steam locomotives here before the house became the secret design centre for Mosquito aircraft. The Hall and garden are open Sundays (Easter day to September) and Thursdays (July to September) 10 30 to 12 30 and 14 00 to 17 30. Admission £1; children 50p (aircraft 50p and 25p). Teas are available at Nell Gwynne's Cottage.

Walk past the lodge and up the drive which leads to Salisbury Hall. At a junction turn right on to a concrete path. Go left (not ahead on to a footpath) with the concrete. Where the cement path bears left again keep ahead along a straight grass bridleway which runs through the University College and Hospital Sports Ground.

On reaching a concrete path go ahead to follow a hedge (right). The concrete gives way to a rough path which bears slightly right with the hedge to go through a wooden gate. After a few yards turn right through a gap to walk down the side of a field. At the far corner go over a wooden stile and keep ahead on a short enclosed path which widens into a metalled drive.

Cross Bell Lane and climb over a wooden stile. Keep to the fence (left) and after about 100 yards bear half right to continue north but on the right side of the field (near a works). To the left there is a view across the sunken bridlepath to the large convent chapel of All Saints – designed by Comper in 1927.

At the far end of the field go over a wooden stile and keep forward along a line of trees (right) to cross a stream. Do not cross the River Colne footbridge but turn right to pass a row of houses and reach the road bridge and ford in London Colney.

LONDON COLNEY. Apart from the buildings by the river most of the village has been developed recently. The church of St. Peter, near the old buildings, was built in 1825 when the parish was created.

Do not cross the river but go over the main road to pass the

'Bull' (right) and walk down Lowbell Lane. Follow the lane, which runs under the London Colney by-pass, and ignore all turnings. Beyond a farm the way runs up to an iron gate. Ahead is a clear view of Tyttenhanger Park.

TYTTENHANGER. The original house, built in 1410, was a retreat for the Abbot of St. Albans. Henry VIII and Catherine of Aragon stayed here during an outbreak of plague in London. At the Dissolution, the building passed to Sir Thomas Pope, founder of Trinity College Oxford, who held the future Queen Elizabeth prisoner at nearby Hatfield. The present house, designed either by Inigo Jones or Peter Mills, was built in 1654 for Sir Henry Blount, who had written *Voyage of the Levant* in 1636. There is a chapel on the second floor and Elizabethan panelling in the attic. An early visitor was John Evelyn. The house is now occupied by offices and Henry Blount's ghost is said to appear in the study.

Bear half right across the field to meet the concrete driveway in the far corner (where there may be wire to negotiate). Do not go over the cattle grid but leave the drive to go down the side of the field with a wood to the left. Bear left with the edge of the field to meet a stile by wooden gates. Go ahead over the stile and through Garden Wood. A notice warns against straying from the path. Ignore a cross path and keep forward on the indistinct way which narrows between holly bushes. Climb over a stile and keep ahead. After a few yards the fence to the right falls away and the path continues forward across a wide open field.

On reaching a house, go to the left of the building to cross a double stile. Walk past the house (right) and across a field to go through an iron gate (right) in the corner. Continue in the north-east direction across an open field. On the far side cross a ditch and go ahead. There is a glimpse of a windmill (without sails) to the right. Cross a narrow stile ahead and bear half right through the bushes on Colney Heath to reach a road by a bridge.

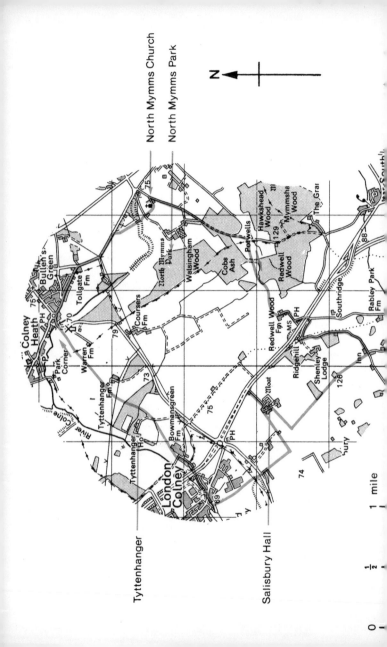

N

North Mymms Church
North Mymms Park
Tyttenhanger
Salisbury Hall

0   ½   1 mile

Turn left to go over the bridge and follow the road to a cross-roads in the centre of Colney Heath village.

Go right to walk along Tollgate Road. Beyond a bus shelter the road bears half right by Tollgate Farm. Later the road bears half left and begins to go downhill. After a short distance turn right over a stile. There is a view of the North Mymms Park mansion.

NORTH MYMMS PARK. In 1554 the future Elizabeth I stayed a night at the earlier building when she was taken from Ashridge to the Tower. The present house, known locally as 'Little Hatfield', was built at the end of the 16th century by Sir Ralph Coningsby. When his grandson was sent to the Tower for supporting Charles I the house was plundered. Later it passed to Sir Thomas Hyde and then the Duke of Leeds. There were several owners until the 1890s when the house was purchased by Mr. Walter Hayes Burns. On his death Mrs. Burns travelled around Europe with her brother, John Pierpont Morgan (the American banker and art collector) and together they filled the house with books, rare tapestries and other antiques. In 1979 Mrs. Burns' grandson, Major-General Sir George Burns, put the contents up for sale and the auction, conducted by Christie's, fetched over £2½ million. The building, one of the best surviving examples of a late Elizabethan house, was sold to an architect.

Walk through the trees and head towards the left side of the house (in the distance). After about 100 yards bear half left – keeping a long wire fence to the left and two clumps of trees to the right. Go over a wooden stile and cross a wooden footbridge spanning the infant River Colne which often flows in swallow holes beneath ground (see River Mole page 79). Keep ahead, crossing (by stiles) the North Mymms Park drive, to reach a churchyard in the trees. Cross a wooden stile and go through the kissing-gate which are both opposite the church's west door.

NORTH MYMMS CHURCH. St. Mary's is mainly 14th century and has an Elizabethan pulpit. Nick Faldo, the golfer, was married here. The vicarage (north) is 17th-century and the wrought iron screen (south) marks the private entrance to the mansion's garden, designed by Sir Ernest George in the 19th century.

Walk past the church (left) and leave the churchyard by Church Cottage (right) to follow the drive to a junction. Turn right to walk southwards along the metalled lane which follows a holly hedge (right).

Where the metalled way swings to the right keep ahead up a rough enclosed path. The path rises through a felled area to Cangsley Grove. On emerging into the open go downhill through an archway of trees to leave the way by turning right at the bottom, and walk westwards up the sloping field to find a small gate on the far side. (Local walkers tend to bear right earlier, at the top of the hill, and walk along the top of the field, through a gap into the next field, to find the small gate on the right, set back from the path).

Beyond the gate go ahead to follow the side of Redwell Wood (left) which, after 350 yards, bears left to an iron gate. Follow the enclosed farm track ahead which passes through a second gateway. On approaching Redwell Wood Farm leave the track, which bears left, and keep ahead to a stile. Cross the stile and a fence to walk through the farm. Follow the metalled drive which, beyond the farmhouse (right), bears right. There is a view of South Mimms Church (which has launched a £30,000 repair appeal) to the left. At a junction, before the 'Waggon and Horses', go left to walk down to the main road. A bus stop is to the left (for Barnet) and another opposite (for St. Albans).

The walk continues on the far side of the dual carriageway. Go ahead to the top of Packhorse Lane. Turn right and follow the lane up the slope and round a bend (by a post box). The lane runs downhill to pass a white cottage (right) and, after just over ¼ mile, the lane passes Pinks Hotel (right).

Just beyond Pinks Cottage (left) turn right to walk down a

narrow path at the side of a wooden gate (left) and to follow a
wooden fence (left) to a stile. Beyond the stile follow a footpath to
reach a track. Go left on to the enclosed track. Soon there is a view
(half right) of Shenley Lodge. After nearly $\frac{1}{4}$ mile the way runs up
to a stile (near a gate). Go ahead over the stile and walk up to the top
of the hill where there is a fine view. To the left there is a hospital
chimney and ahead St. Albans Cathedral (see page 28).

Keep ahead over the brow of the hill and down through a clump
of trees to reach two stiles. Cross the stiles and keep heading north
by the small wood (right) which soon gives way to open country.
There is a view of Salisbury Hall (half right).

Go over a stile by a gateway and continue following the wire
fence (right). Beyond a second gateway turn right to walk up to
Salisbury Hall. Beyond a barn go through a gateway and turn left
and right to reach the drive which leads to the main road and bus
stop.

7 End of the Line

ONGAR – GREENSTED – TOOTHILL – NORTH WEALD BASSETT –
COOPERSALE COMMON – EPPING
$2\frac{1}{2}$, 5 or $8\frac{3}{4}$ MILES

THE CENTRAL Line was extended from Loughton to Ongar in 1865
and because money was short the line had to follow the contours of
the land. The area is still rural and recently a tube driver was
attacked by a rabbit when he stopped his train at the isolated Blake
Hall Station. Until 1957 trains were steam-hauled on the
Epping–Ongar section which remains a single line. This walk is
never far from one of the stations and joins Walk 8 to make a
16-mile route.

ONGAR: Underground (Central Line). Bus 247B (Mondays to Saturdays). London Country Bus 339.

BLAKE HALL: Underground (Central Line).

NORTH WEALD: Underground (Central Line). London Country Bus 339.

COOPERSALE: G. F. Ward Bus 381 (Mondays to Saturdays).

EPPING: Underground (Central Line). Bus 20A, 247. London Country Bus 329, 339. Green Line Coach 702, 712, 713 (Mondays to Saturdays). G. F. Ward Bus 381 (Mondays to Saturdays).

CHIPPING ONGAR. At the end of Castle Street there are the earthworks of a Norman castle where Richard de Lucy (who founded Lesnes Abbey; see page 94) lived. A market grew up at the gate – 'Chipping' is derived from 'Chepe', meaning market. The church was built about the same time and restored in 1884. Oliver Cromwell's cousin, Jane, is buried under the altar. Edward Boodle, founder of 'Boodles' is buried on the south side of the churchyard. Jane Taylor, who wrote 'Twinkle, Twinkle Little Star', lived at Castle House from 1811 to 1829 when her father was the Congregational Minister. In 1838 David Livingstone, who trained under Mr. Taylor's successor, lived in the room above the archway in front of the United Reformed Church (then the Congregational Church). It was from here that he wrote to the London Missionary Society asking to be allowed to go to Africa. He is commemorated in stained glass in the north wall of the Anglican church.

On leaving the station walk up to the main road and turn right. Walk down Bansons Lane, opposite the 'Cock'. At the bottom of the hill, cross the Cripsey Brook and keep ahead (ignoring the concrete path half left). The wide footpath ahead was an avenue of elms until the mid-1970s. Towards the end of the path there is a glimpse of Blake Hall to the right.

BLAKE HALL is early 18th-century but the wings were added about 1840. The house gave its name to the nearby station.

Go through the swing gate ahead and cross the drive of the (partly Elizabethan) Greensted Hall to reach a second swing gate. Keep ahead (towards the buildings) to go through another swing gate by a field gate. On the far side of the second field go through a gate by a pond (left). Keep ahead up the metalled drive to reach the church.

GREENSTED – JUXTA – ONGAR. The Saxon church, built about 1013, is the world's oldest log church. The body of St. Edmund is said to have rested here on its way to Bury St. Edmunds. The tower is probably 14th-century. During the Tudor period the chancel was rebuilt and the thatch replaced with tiles. The building was carefully restored by the Reverend Philip Ray who objected to the Tolpuddle Martyrs moving into the parish after their free pardon and return from Australia. Although Ray had described the Dorset farmworkers as 'convicts' he conducted the wedding here of James Brine (the only Anglican Tolpuddle Martyr) and the daughter of his fellow Martyr Thomas Standfield. In 1972 the church appeared on the 3p stamp as part of the special 'village churches' issue. John Garrington, Rector from 1963 to 1978, was married to the Reverend Elsie Chamberlain, the Congregationalist.

Turn right to walk through the farmyard of Hall Farm. Follow the farm track ahead and where the way divides keep left to reach a gateway. Beyond the gate go right to walk uphill across a field. At a second gateway, where the path swings to the left, keep ahead up the side of a field and bear left in front of two cottages (New Barns). Go right, down the side of a cottage garden, to cross a wooden footbridge and meet a cross-path.

Turn left to follow the wooded path, known as Pensons Lane. On reaching a cottage (right) the way becomes metalled. Just beyond a brick house (Silver Birch; left) there is a lane which leads past Tudor Cottage.

TUDOR COTTAGE was formerly New House Farm and had 80

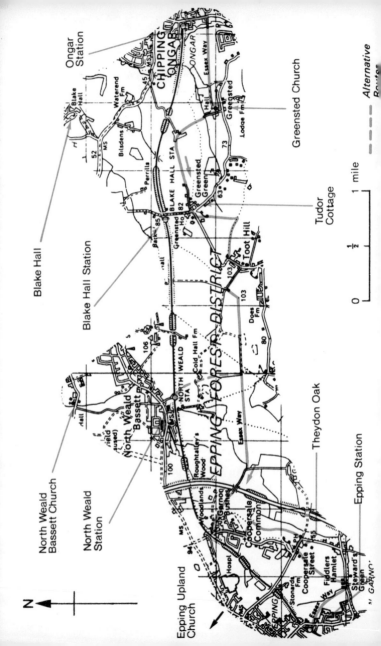

N

Ongar Station

Blake Hall

Blake Hall Station

North Weald Bassett Church

North Weald Station

Epping Upland Church

Greensted Church

Tudor Cottage

Theydon Oak

Epping Station

Alternative Routes

acres attached. From 1838 this was the home of Tolpuddle Martyrs George and James Loveless who moved in with their families and James Brine, who was soon able to describe himself on the marriage certificate as a 'farmer' (see above). Martyr James Hammett joined them in August 1839 and stayed until 1841. A deposit for the farm and Fenners Farm (at nearby Magdalen Laver) had been paid by public subscription and in 1839 a benefit evening at London's Old Vic helped to purchase the lease on both farms. George Loveless formed the Greensted Chartist Association and large meetings were held in the barn which can be seen just beyond the cottage. Delegates came to gatherings from all over Essex and Hertfordshire including Waltham Abbey, Epping and Harlow. However, the vicar wrote to the Chelmsford Magistrates and the Lord Lieutenant complaining about this activity and when the attacks were taken up in the newspapers the Martyrs, fearful of being held responsible for any trouble in the area, decided to emigrate to Canada in 1844. The plaque was unveiled in 1976 in the presence of Len Murray, TUC General Secretary.

The walk continues down Pensons Lane to reach a cross-roads. The road to the right leads to Blake Hall Station. The walk continues ahead up the Toot Hill Road. After passing the gothick Ivy Cottage (right) go left at the entrance to a new house. Walk up the side of a new garden to follow a hedge (right) up and then downhill. Where the hedge ends go ahead to cross a stile and a footbridge. Continue ahead uphill towards a cluster of concrete signposts (which can be seen on the horizon) to pass two solitary trees (right).

At the top of the hill cross a ditch by the signposts and turn right. On reaching the corner of the field follow a short woodland path to reach another field. Go right along the side of the field to cross a footbridge. Keep ahead towards the houses with a ditch to the right. On approaching the buildings bear right across the ditch to go up the side of the buildings and turn left over a stile.

Walk ahead to join a road at a bend. Keep forward up the road through Toot Hill for 250 yards and, before reaching the green, go right up a lane.

There is a glimpse of a water tower. On reaching the tower and the white Clunes House (left) continue ahead through a gateway and (before a tank) turn left.

Follow a track which curves gently to the right with the edge of the large field. When the trees (left) fall away keep ahead. The unfenced track gently rises and then runs downhill through a wood (the remains of Ongar Park Wood). On leaving the wood the path climbs steeply and continues ahead to High Wood.

To reach North Weald Station turn right on entering the wood and follow a path just inside the trees. When the path runs out of the wood keep ahead through a gap and bear half left with trees to the left. (Ahead is a glimpse of North Weald Bassett church tower.) Go through a second gap and bear half right. To the right there is Cold Hall. Go over a gravel drive and follow the path ahead which crosses the railway line by the station.

NORTH WEALD BASSETT. 'Weald' means 'forest' and the Bassett family were 13th-century lords of the manor. The 'King's Head' is Tudor and was once a coaching inn. The church is ¾ mile to the north and has a Tudor tower. The airfield provided fighters for the Battle of Britain.

The walk continues ahead through the wood. The way cuts through a low dyke and beyond double dykes runs into the open. After a short distance the straight path runs through Birching Coppice. When a path joins from the right the path runs along the side of a wooden fence (right). Follow the fence to go over the M11 motorway.

On the far side of the motorway keep ahead on the firm path which runs through a wood known as Garnon Bushes, to meet a metalled lane. Turn left and follow the metalled lane which becomes gravelled just before joining a road.

Go left to pass the 'Garnon Bushes' pub and walk through Coopersale Common. Just before reaching St. Alban's Church (right) turn left between Southview and the church car park.

Walk through the wooden gates and after a short distance (just before the notice on a tree) turn right to follow a path through a wood. The way bends to the right and runs downhill. At the bottom of the slope the path bears left along the edge of the wood. By a field divide turn right over a large tree stump and leave the trees. Follow a hedge (right) and after passing into a second field bear half left across the field to a stile – but walkers usually continue ahead by the hedge (right) and at the corner turn left to find, half way down the field, the stile (right).

Cross the stile and, continue ahead by a gate and hedge (right). At the end of the field go through the iron gate and keep forward to cross a stile and follow a short path to a road and Coopersale Street.

Turn right and just beyond the 'Theydon Oak' (right) and a barn (left) go left up a rough lane known as Steward's Green Lane. Pass the entrance to High Meadow (right) and beyond a wooden gate (right) the way narrows and becomes enclosed to run through trees and undergrowth for ½ mile. On joining a wide track, continue forward to pass through a row of cottages and meet a road.

Turn right and beyond two cottages go right through a gateway. Keep ahead round the edge (right) of the field. The way follows a ditch (right). After the path turns right and crosses the ditch, bear half left up a firm path. On leaving the field go ahead up an enclosed path to reach a road.

Turn right up the hill and go left into Hillcrest Way which leads to Epping Station.

EPPING. 'Ep' means 'up' and 'ing' a 'forest clearing'. The late Victorian church of St. John the Baptist stands on the site of a Norman chapel which was served by clergy from Waltham Abbey. Until 1888 All Saints at Epping Upland was the parish church. John Overall, Vicar of Epping in 1592–3, became Bishop of Norwich and helped to translate the Authorized Version of the Bible. Henry III granted the town's first market charter and the present Monday market (held on Friday until the First World War) was begun in 1575. Cattle, once walked through the town to Smithfield, were sold at the Monday market until 1961. Henry Doubleday, the 19th-century Quaker naturalist, lived in the grocery shop on the corner of Buttercross Lane.

8 London's Back Garden

EPPING – LOUGHTON – HIGH BEACH – CHINGFORD
$4\frac{3}{4}$ or $7\frac{1}{4}$ MILES

EPPING FOREST, which has been called 'London's back garden', was once part of the Royal Forest of Essex. In 1878 the present 6,000 acres were acquired by the City of London which already owned a farm and a cemetery at Wanstead. There are 4,000 acres of woodland and 150 ponds. 144 different bird species have been seen in the area and the 100 strong herd of Black Fallow Deer (dark brown in colour) is believed to be the oldest in the country. The cattle belong to local people who enjoy commoners' ancient grazing rights. The only memorial allowed in the Forest is near Woodford Green where the birthplace (a tent) of Gypsy Smith, the preacher who died on the 'Queen Mary' during her maiden voyage, is marked by a stone. The present Ranger of Epping Forest is the Duke of Gloucester.

EPPING: Underground (Central Line). Bus 20A, 247. London

Country Bus 329, 339. Green Line 702, 712, 713 (Mondays to Fridays).

GOLDINGS HILL: Bus 20A, 250.

LOUGHTON: Underground (Central Line). Bus 20 20A, 167, 250, 255 (Mondays to Saturdays). Green Line 702.

CHINGFORD: Bus 69, 102, 121 (Mondays to Saturdays), 179, 191 (Mondays to Saturdays), 242. Or British Rail.

EPPING. See page 49.

On leaving Epping Station (main entrance) turn right and, after a few yards, go left up a narrow path by the car park exit. The way bends left and then right, up a partly stepped path, to a road. Turn left and walk along the residential road for $\frac{1}{4}$ mile.

Just over the brow of the hill (where the hedged pavement ends) turn right up Western Avenue. The road bends to the left (round a grassed area) and on the right, beyond No. 29, there is the entrance to a footpath.

Walk along the path and ignore any turnings. Where the way appears to bend to the right, do not follow a path through a barrier but go around the bushes ahead and keep forward on another footpath. Soon the way bears slightly to the right (by a fence) to reach Bell Common.

Turn left to cross a metalled path and follow a line of houses (left) facing the Common. The main road is over to the right. At the far end there is the 'Forest Gate'.

FOREST GATE is a free house which dates from at least the 16th century. It was probably once a toll gate. During the Great Plague of 1665 supplies for Epping were left outside the public house.

Keep ahead for 200 yards and turn right at a road junction (by Ivy Chimney's Road), to walk up a rough track known as Forest

Side. Go forward where the main track turns left and after a few
yards bear half left through the trees to find the top of a broad forest
ride. Walk along the partly gravelled path which becomes firmer
when a path (from Theydon Bois) joins from the left. After a third
dip the trees become less dense to reveal the ridges of Ambersbury
Banks (right).

AMBERSBURY BANKS, an ancient British earthwork, was
thrown up between 300BC and AD10. It is traditionally held to
have been the scene of the last stand of Queen Boadicea against the
Roman General Suetonius.

The way later crosses a road called Jack's Hill which was a
bridlepath in the 19th century. Continue ahead along a path,
known as The Ditches, which dips twice before climbing steeply
to reach a line of houses. Bear slightly right to follow a path which
leaves the houses to reach two new lodges on Goldings Hill. Cross
the main road and go left for about 400 yards. Turn right into
Baldwins Hill. No. 50, on the right is 'Deerhurst'.

DEERHURST AND LITTLE MONKWOOD COTTAGE,
built in 1870 as three homes known as Prospect Cottages, was the
country home of Sir Jacob Epstein from 1933 to 1950. In the 1920s
he had lived at Oak Lodge (No. 49 on the corner of Whitaker Way)
where, in a shed, he had created *Rima* for Hyde Park (See page 100)
and *The Visitation*, which is now in the Tate Gallery. He painted
hundreds of watercolours of the forest where he had hoped that
one of his sculptures would stand permanently. In 1934 a London
Transport poster featured one of his Epping Forest paintings. After
1950 Epstein lived at his London home in Hyde Park Gate.

Walk past the 'Forest Arms' (left) and a further row of houses to
the right.

To reach Loughton and Loughton Station keep ahead. Pass St. John's
Road and follow the now narrow road round a bend. Before reaching the
'Gardener's Arms' bear right on a metalled footpath which crosses Wood-

bury Hill to join York Hill. Continue down the road to turn right at the
main road by the 'King's Head'. Just beyond the Church of St. Mary the
Virgin go left to pass Lopping Hall (right) and reach Loughton Station.

LOUGHTON was the centre of the struggle to preserve Epping Forest.
For years local woodcutters had enjoyed an ancient right to cut firewood
and proclaimed their rights each Lopping Day, 11 November, by lighting
a fire on Staple's Hill at midnight. However, in 1865 the Reverend John
Maitland, a landowner and the Rector of Loughton, fenced in 1,300 acres
to sell to developers. A large banquet with plenty of ale was staged at the
'King's Head' on the evening of 10 November in the hope that the
woodcutters would be too drunk to perform the annual ceremony
confirming their rights. However, 73-year-old Tom Willingale stayed
sober and slipped out just before midnight to perform the ritual. He
returned to brandish a branch before the furious landowners. The legal
battle against the developers lasted years and won the support of the
City of London who, under the 1878 Epping Forest Act, now administer
the Forest – Lopping Hall, which has an interesting sculpture above the
door, was built in the 1880s with part of the £7,000 paid by the City of
London for the ancient Lopping Rights. St. Nicholas, the old village
church in Rectory Lane (near Debden Station), was rebuilt in 1877 but
inside there are brasses and a pair of kneeling Tudor figures from the earlier
building. Sarah Martin, who wrote 'Old Mother Hubbard' and attracted
William IV, is buried in the churchyard between a Victorian replica of
Edward the Confessor's shrine (in Westminster Abbey) and the road.
Loughton Hall, next to St. Nicholas, was built in 1878 and succeeds an
Inigo Jones house. Trap's Hill (opposite the Methodist Church) is said to
be haunted by Dick Turpin, who drags a woman behind his horse.

The walk continues to the right, beyond the row of houses
(right) in Baldwins Hill. A narrow track known as Clay Road runs
downhill to pass a pond (right). The gently rising path meets a
gravel cross path. Keep ahead to reach, after ½ mile, Epping New
Road. Climb up the bank opposite and beyond a cross path bear a
quarter left and reach a wooden fence. Turn left and then right with
the fence to reach a road at High Beach.

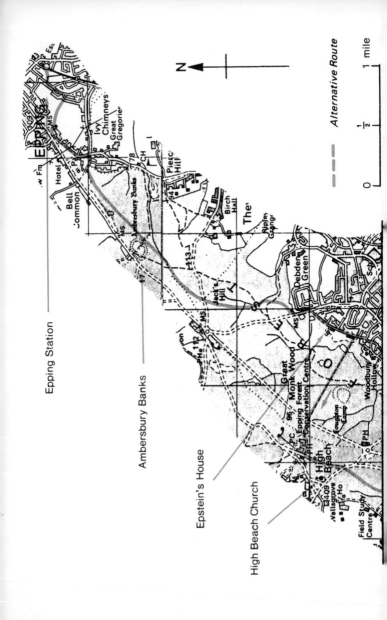

Epping Station

Ambersbury Banks

Epstein's House

High Beach Church

N

0   ½   1 mile

– – – Alternative Route

N

St. Nicholas' Church

Loughton Station

St. John the Baptist Church

Chingford Bus & British Rail Stations

Chingford Old Church

Queen Elizabeth's Hunting Lodge

LOUGHTON

CHINGFORD

Long Hills

Whitehouse Plain

The Warren

Queen Elizabeth's Hunting Lodge

tonebury

- - - - Alternative Route

0   ½   1 mile

A   B

HIGH BEACH means 'gravel bank'. Tennyson lived at Beach Hill Park (to the north) in the 1830s when mourning Hallam's death and too poor to marry. The poet, in his blue coat, would skate on the pond. Whilst here he worked on *In Memoriam*, *The Talking Oak*, *Locksley Hall* and *Ring Out, Wild Bells* (of nearby Waltham Abbey). An exploding fireball, which left his mother rolling and sobbing on the floor, led to Tennyson's departure in 1840. The church, by Sir Arthur Blomfield, was built in 1873 to succeed an old chapel and the parish was created in 1884. It was here, in 1882, that Queen Victoria said 'It gives me the greatest satisfaction to dedicate this beautiful forest for the use and enjoyment of my people for all time'.

To the right there is the 'King's Oak'. The walk continues to the left along the road. At a junction turn left and after a few yards go right to find a path beyond two logs. The woodland path bends left and after ¼ mile runs into the open. At a junction go right and then left with the main gravel path which soon runs through more woodland. Keep ahead at a junction. Where the path rises keep left with the main path to follow the way ahead (known as Magpie Hill). Beyond a cross path the way runs into the open and there is a view of Chingford to the right.

Where the way divides leave the gravel and keep forward up a wide grass path with a view of St. John the Baptist church at Buckhurst Hill to the left. On reaching a white weather-boarded refreshment house, once a 19th-century barn, turn right along the road to pass Queen Elizabeth's Hunting Lodge.

QUEEN ELIZABETH'S HUNTING LODGE which now houses a forest museum, was built by Henry VIII. The Royal party in the (then open) galleries would shoot at the herds of deer driven towards the building. Elizabeth I is said to have ridden her horse up the stairs to celebrate the Spanish Armada's defeat. William Morris was brought here as a child in the 1840s and later recalled the impression of romance made on him by one of the rooms. The

Royal Forest Hotel, next door, was built in 1880 although most of the present structure dates from the 1930s – the garage is the original coach house. The Hunting Lodge is open Wednesdays to Sundays 14 00 to 18 00 (or dusk if earlier), admission 10p.

Continue along the main road to pass the Royal Forest Hotel (right) and reach the railway and bus station at Chingford.

CHINGFORD comes from the 13th-century 'Chagingeford' meaning 'the ford of dwellers by stumps'. The church on the Green was designed by Vulliamy and built in 1844 at the expense of the Rector who lived at Friday Hill House (now the Community and Arts Centre) in Simmons Lane. This house (redesigned by Vulliamy) is where James I, having enjoyed a good dinner, is said to have laid his sword on the roast beef and dubbed it 'Sir Loin'. The 12th-century parish church (Chingford Old Church) is a mile to the south-west in Old Church Road (Bus 69). It was raided by Dick Turpin who found that the churchwardens had taken the plate home. Arthur Hughes's painting *Home from the Sea* (in the Ashmolean Museum, Oxford) shows the church in the 19th century. Lawrence of Arabia owned Pole Hill where he occasionally camped. Queen Victoria used Chingford station when she went to High Beach (see page 56) in 1882. The bus station stands on the site of the railway coal yard.

9 Beyond The Southend Road

UPMINSTER — GREAT WARLEY — CHILDERDITCH — THORNDON PARK —
BRENTWOOD
8 MILES

AS EASTERN AVENUE becomes the Southend Arterial Road, on its way to the 'East Enders' Brighton', the A127 begins to run through the Essex countryside. Upminster Station, first used by the underground in 1902, was originally part of the London, Tilbury and Southend Railway. This walk crosses the teeming traffic and visits the unspoilt hills and hamlets on the north side of the famous road and railway. The only pubs and cafés are in Upminster and Brentwood but there are seats for picnics in Thorndon Park.

UPMINSTER PARK ESTATE: Underground (District Line) then bus 248 to Front Lane.

GREAT WARLEY: London Country Bus 369 (Mondays to Saturdays).

BRENTWOOD: Bus 247, London Country Bus 369 (Mondays to Saturdays). Or British Rail which connects with the Underground (Central Line) at Stratford.

UPMINSTER means 'church on higher ground'. The present church of St. Laurence has a 13th-century tower. The former Rectory, next door, dates from 1765. The windmill was built in 1803–4. Upminster Hall, north of the station, is Elizabethan and the nearby Tithe Barn is now the Agricultural and Folk Museum (open first weekend of summer months; admission free). The 18th-century Clock House was once a stables and coach house.

Leave the bus (248) in Front Lane and continue northwards along the road to pass a garage (left). Just between a house called Bonanza (left) and an older house, go left up a narrow enclosed path. Climb over a wooden stile and continue ahead along the side (right) of a field to cross a temporary stile at the far corner. Keep forward through some bushes to enter another field. After crossing a ditch go ahead near the side of the field (left) to go over a wooden stile at the far end of the field.

Walk up the slope to follow a path ahead. When the trees (left) fall away keep ahead (towards a house in the distance) across the strawberry field to join Bird Lane at a bend. Turn left along the lane to pass a row of houses and after a short distance there is a stile on the right. Cross the stile and keep ahead along a line of trees (right). Go up a slope and down through a copse to cross, at the end of a hollow, a stile by the dual carriageway (to Southend).

Cross the main road *with care* and climb over a (partly hidden) stile. Keep forward along the side (left) of a field to cross another stile. Continue ahead up the side (left) of a second field and at the corner go through the trees to reach a metalled drive (leading to Upminster Lodge Farm). Go right on to Tomkins Lane and turn left. After 200 yards, by the entrance to the 15th-century Great Tomkyns (left), turn right up an enclosed path.

Continue ahead beyond a stile to go over a stile by a gate. Keep forward, with views to the left and right, through an iron gate and past a pond (left). Beyond another gate the way runs downhill and bears round to the right. Keep by the fence (right) and cross the stile at the end. Continue ahead by a line of trees (right) which give way to a fence. Follow the fence (right) down to a stile at Beredens Lane.

Turn right to pass two cottages (right). Beyond a slope leave the road to go through a gate (left). Bear $\frac{1}{4}$ right to reach the end of the line of trees ahead. (Work on the new M25 will begin here shortly). Follow the ditch (left) to go over a footbridge by the stiles. Continue forward with the fence (right) and cross another stile. Keep

by the fence (right) and at the next corner go left towards Hole
Farm. Cross a wooden stile by the side of the iron gate to walk
through the farm.

Beyond the buildings cross a stile and walk through a field to
cross a stile by an iron gate. Bear round to the left to join a metalled
path and follow the way up the hill. Soon there is a view of the spire
on Great Warley Church. On reaching the road turn left to the
church.

GREAT WARLEY CHURCH. St. Mary's, built 1902–4, is a
complete *art nouveau* church. The building was designed by
Charles Harrison Townsend who had been responsible for the
Whitechapel Art Gallery and the Horniman Museum. On the spire
there is a huge dove which looks like a parrot.

On reaching the church turn right up an enclosed path at the side
of Rectory Lodge. Keep forward along the side (right) of a field and
on entering a second field bear ¼ left downhill to cross a stream at a
footbridge. Climb over a stile and go up the hill to pass the side of a
farm. Cross a stile by a gate to reach a lane near a junction with
Magpie Lane.

Turn right along Bird Lane (with the golf course to the left) and
follow the road which soon runs downhill to cross a stream. Just
before the stream leave the lane and bear half left to follow the
stream (right). Cross a footbridge (over another stream) and bear
right with the main stream to reach a field. (An unofficial path
continues along the stream to a cross path). Bear half left up the
field. Soon a house (St. Peter's Rectory) comes into view. Head
towards the house, passing a field corner (right) and a pond, to go
over a broken stile and cross a gravelled drive.

Go ahead through a wooden gateway and follow the high hedge
(left). Ahead there is a view of the early 18th-century tower of St.
Peter's, Little Warley. Go through a gap into a second field. Do not
bear left with a farm track but keep ahead until the field boundary
on the left gives way and the field opens out. Here bear half left

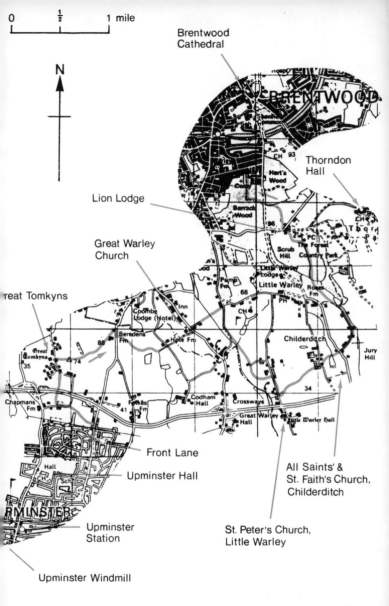

0   ½   1 mile

N

Brentwood Cathedral

BRENTWOOD

Thorndon Hall

Lion Lodge

Great Warley Church

Great Tomkyns

All Saints' & St. Faith's Church, Childerditch

Front Lane

Upminster Hall

St. Peter's Church, Little Warley

Upminster Station

UPMINSTER

Upminster Windmill

across to the far corner. Cross a footbridge to reach (opposite the
end of a row of houses) Little Warley Hall Lane.

Turn right and just beyond the Kelrose Swimpool Centre (right)
the lane crosses a stream. At once turn left over a stile and follow
the side (left) of a large field. Ahead is a view of a farm and the
church of All Saints & St. Faith's, Childerditch. (The church was
rebuilt in the 19th century but has a Tudor font. Poet Edward
Thomas wrote about the area).

On approaching the farm keep forward up an enclosed way
leading to the centre of the buildings. Turn right and left to walk
through a barn and reach a road opposite Childerditch Hall.

Turn left for a short distance and just past The Cottage (right) go
right through an iron gate. Bear half left down the hill to pass a
newly created lake (right). Beyond the lake is the church. At the
side of the lake go through an iron gate and ahead up the hill
towards a wooden gate. Keep to the right of the gate to follow the
side (left) of a garden and go over a wooden stile to reach Childerditch Lane.

Cross the lane and go ahead up Childerditch Street. Beyond a
farm the way bears left to run northwards. Where the metalled
surface ends continue ahead to pass Childerditch Pond (right).

On reaching an iron gate keep on the right to continue forward
on a bridleway at the side of Childerditch Wood (right). This path
is part of Thorndon Country Park.

THORNDON COUNTRY PARK. The house of Thorndon
Park was mentioned in the Domesday Book and the park was
created for deer in 1414 with the permission of Henry V. During
Elizabeth I's reign the estate was bought by the Petre family who
remained Roman Catholic. The fourth Lord Petre died in the
Tower of London in 1684 after being falsely implicated in the
Popish Plot. The eighth baron, featured in Pope's *Rape of The
Lock* lived at Ingatestone but in the 1730s his son moved back to

Thorndon and grew pineapples, bananas and limes in colossal hot-houses. Before his death at only 29 he had introduced the Camellia to England and employed Bourginion to landscape the gardens. A fatherless son was left and on growing up he abandoned the house in the 1760s for a new mansion (which included a Catholic chapel) designed by James Paine. At huge cost 'Capability' Brown landscaped the grounds. Lord Petre, in spite of his Catholicism, was visited by George III and Queen Charlotte when the King was inspecting troops nearby. A hundred years later a fire ended the family's occupation of the 18th-century house which remained derelict until 1979 when work begun on converting the building into 85 flats. The nearby Petre mausoleum and chantry chapel, designed by Pugin, remains to the west of the house.

At a junction keep forward round a bend to pass another pond (right) and after 100 yards go through an iron gate and over a cross path. Keep ahead up the slope ahead into a plantation known as The Forest. At a junction turn left and then right to continue north. The growth to the right is known as the Laurel Plantation. At the third cross path turn left to pass the toilet block (right). At a second cross path (beyond the barrier) turn right and follow the bridleway to meet the main metalled path by the Lion Lodge (left).

LION LODGE was the entrance to the western carriage drive to the 18th-century mansion (see above).

Turn left to go through the gateway and reach a road. Cross the road and either take the left-hand bridlepath or the right footpath (edged with logs). The footpath winds ahead through Kent's Wood to cross a footbridge by a barrier. At once pass a second footbridge (right) and follow a ditch (right) to reach a road (where the bridlepath joins from the left).

Turn right along the road for 10 yards to go left across the road and follow another path through Donkey Lane Plantation. After $\frac{1}{4}$ mile turn right up a straight path which later runs through a fence and into the residential Guardsman Close.

At a T-junction, near the 'Brave Nelson' (right), turn left and
follow the road to meet Warley Hill in Brentwood. There are bus
stops to the left by the 'Prince Albert' and the Brentwood Station is
down the hill to the right.

BRENTWOOD means 'burnt wood'. A hamlet grew up in the
area destroyed by fire and a chapel (now a ruin in the High Street)
was founded by monks. Pilgrims to St. Thomas à Becket's shrine at
Canterbury visited here on their way from Pilgrims Hatch to the
ferry at Tilbury. The recently enlarged St. Helen's Cathedral was
built in 1861 (with the help of Lord Petre) as a chapel and became a
cathedral in 1917 when the new Roman Catholic Diocese was
formed. Brentwood School (opposite the Cathedral) was founded
during Elizabeth I's reign.

10 Valley of Vision

SWANLEY — EYNSFORD — SHOREHAM — EYNSFORD — SWANLEY
12 or 5 MILES

THOSE WHO embark on the longer route can always curtail the
walk, after only 5¾ miles, at Shoreham where there are buses and
trains.

The Darenth valley was well known to London's hop-pickers
until the mid-1950s when the Garden of England opted for
mechanized labour. Arthur Mee described the area as 'probably
unique on the map of rural England', and Samuel Palmer called it
the 'Valley of Vision'. The local population is split as to whether
the M25 should be cut through this unspoilt countryside – Lord
David Cecil, Yehudi Menuhin and many ramblers say 'No', but
some villagers who live on the main Eynsford road would like to
see the traffic diverted from their front doors.

SWANLEY: Bus 21A. Green Line Coach 729 (Mondays to Fridays). Or British Rail.

EYNSFORD: London Country Bus 400 (Mondays to Fridays), 401 (Mondays to Saturdays), 456 (Sundays). Or British Rail.

SHOREHAM: London Country Bus 404 (Mondays to Saturdays), 421 (Mondays to Saturdays), 456 (Sundays). Or British Rail.

SWANLEY has developed since the railway came here. The original village, to the north, dates from the Saxon period although the church is only Victorian. A cedar tree at Highlands Farm was planted in 1815 to commemorate the Battle of Waterloo. The Church of St. Mary The Virgin, in Maidstone Road at Swanley Junction, still maintains the high church tradition which caused arrows and 'This way to Rome' to be daubed on the outside walls after its opening in 1901. Henry Cannell, who discovered the scarlet geranium, lived at Swanley Junction.

On arriving at Swanley bus garage, walk ahead. Keep to the right side of the road. When the houses end the road bends to the right to cross the by-pass and then left to cross the top of Wested Lane. Keep ahead to pass an isolated row of houses and follow the pavement (which has two breaks for the projected M25) round the edge of a vast roundabout.

On reaching a road junction, follow the pavement up a dual carriageway. After some distance leave the road and turn on to a metalled footpath which runs parallel to the road. The way becomes rough before reaching a junction of paths opposite Button Street.

Turn right to pass a small tree plantation (left) and follow a straight track across open country. The way passes a water tank (right) and two cottages (left). Just beyond the building there is a cross path and a view down the Darenth valley. Go left along another straight unfenced path to walk towards a wood. Keep ahead on a narrow woodland path to reach a seat at the viewpoint on Eynsford Hill.

EYNSFORD HILL. In 1914 Arthur Mee, editor of *The Children's Newspaper* and author of *The King's England*, built a house called 'Eynsford Hill' (the grey building) here. Commenting on the view Mee wrote 'we may see a straight mile probably unique on the map of rural England, beginning with the site of a Roman house, passing a Norman castle, and ending at the site of a Saxon settlement; then if we lengthen our mile a little, heading on to a Tudor gateway in Lullingstone Park. Roman, Norman, Saxon, Tudor – it is all in line, and in sight from Eynsford Hill'.

Turn right to go over a stile and follow a narrow path. To the right is 'Eynsford Hill' and its garden. The way runs downhill and across the drive. On reaching a second drive go left down to a road. Turn left, and on reaching Bridport Cottage garage (left) turn right to find the entrance to a footpath by The Cottage. Follow a hedged way to Sparepenny Lane.

SPAREPENNY LANE, described by Arthur Mee as 'one of the loveliest in Kent', is said to derive its name from the time when the poor would use this route to avoid the penny toll on the main Farningham–Eynsford road.

Go right to a junction by Toll Bar Cottage. The centre of Eynsford is to the left.

EYNSFORD. The church of St. Martin has Norman origins and a 13th-century tower. In 1163, when the patrons failed to fill a vacancy, Thomas à Becket appointed a new priest and excommunicated William de Eynsford who rejected the nominee. This caused the first breach between the primate and Henry II. The villagers forced William out of Eynsford after the murder of Thomas. William's home, which incorporates Roman materials, is the best example of an early castle in the country. The ruins are open 09 30 to 19 00 (17 30 March, April and October; 16 00

November to February). Admission 30p, children and pensioners 15p. The bridge, opposite the church, was used as a pulpit by John Wesley (see Shoreham below). Graham Sutherland lived at Willow Cottage, opposite the 'Malt Shovel' in the early 1930s.

The walk continues to the right – avoiding the centre of the village. *Walkers on the shorter route should bear right off the road before the bridge; see page 72.*

The lane runs under the railway viaduct (built in 1862) and after ¾ mile reaches Lullingstone Roman Villa.

LULLINGSTONE ROMAN VILLA was discovered in the mid-18th century when a fence was being erected. Systematic excavation began in 1949 and revealed, according to Nikolaus Pevsner, 'one of the most interesting Roman show-pieces in the country'. The house dates from about AD80. Between 200 and 280 it was abandoned and became derelict. Late in the 3rd century a Roman family moved in and began rebuilding. Towards the end of the 4th century (200 years before St. Augustine arrived) the family embraced the Christian faith and turned a room into a chapel. There was a disastrous fire in the 5th century and over the years the creeping clay hill behind covered the remains of the house. Open 09 30 to 19 00 (17 30 March, April and October; 16 00 November to February). Admission 60p (40p winter), children and pensioners 30p (20p winter).

The lane beyond the Roman Villa leads to Lullingstone Castle.

LULLINGSTONE CASTLE. *St. Botolph's, known as 'the church on the lawn', dates from the Norman period. The screen inside was erected for Sir John Peche in the 16th century and the carving includes peach stones. The castle gatehouse is Tudor and Catherine of Aragon frequently stayed at the Castle which is now mainly 18th-century. Inside there is a wide staircase built for Queen Anne, whose travelling chests and doll are still here. Above the stairs hangs a lantern from Whitehall Palace. In 1728 Sir Thomas Dyke, the second baronet, married Anne Hart, a descendant of*

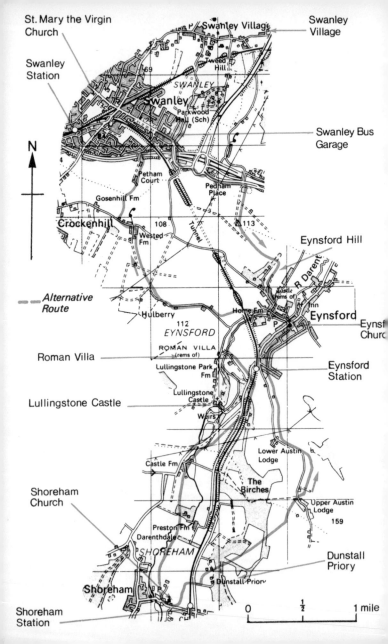

Peche. In 1873 Sir William Hart Dyke, the seventh baronet and Chief
Secretary for Ireland in Disraeli's government, drew up the rules for lawn
tennis when the first ever match was played here. In 1932 Zoë, Lady Hart
Dyke, established a silk farm which provided silk for the Queen's Corona-
tion robe. (The farm, unique in Europe, moved to Hertfordshire and is
now at Compton House in Dorset). The church is open daily (walk
through the gatehouse). The Castle is open April to September on
Wednesdays, Saturdays, Sundays and Bank Holidays 14 00 to 18 00.
Admission 75p, children 15p and pensioners 25p.

To continue the walk go left by the Roman Villa and cross the
River Darent. Follow the partly metalled lane past a cottage (left)
and farm. The 'Private' notice, beyond the gateway, refers to the
field and not the lane. On reaching a gateway by the main road go
right. (There is sometimes a mobile tea stall in the lay-by). Follow
the road up hill and past the northern entrance to Lullingstone
Castle (where the stage coach carrying Samuel Palmer broke
down; see below). After a short distance take the lane on the right –
a signpost points to Castle Farm.

Beyond the river the road bends left to pass Castle Farm and its
miniature windmill. Where the road bends sharply to the right
keep ahead. The footpath runs along the top of a bank above a hop
field (left). At the far end go through a gap to cross a field and reach
a concrete farm road. Go ahead over two stiles and bear half left
across a field to pass an isolated stile. Keep forward to the far corner
and go over a stile by a gateway. Stay by the wire fence on the left.
On reaching another stile (before the end of the field) follow a
footpath by the river.

The path leads to the end of a lane. Turn left and then right to
follow a narrow metalled path to a footbridge. Beyond the bridge
go right to walk along a riverside path. At the end of a brick wall
(left) is Water House (see below) and Shoreham.

SHOREHAM means 'home in the cleft' and until the Reformation
the manor was in the possession of the Archbishop of Canterbury.
The church dates from the 12th century but is mainly Tudor. The

pulpit and organ case are from Westminster Abbey. Burne-Jones designed the window in memory of Joseph Prestwick, the geologist who lived at Darenthulme (behind Darenth Hulme Cottage in Shacklands Road). The churchyard yews were planted in 1867 and the brick path was laid in 1881. Harold Copping, the Bible illustrator who lived at The Studio in Crown Road, and Lord Dunsany, the poet and playwright who lived at Dunstall Priory (see below), are buried to the north-west of the church. John Wesley, a friend of the vicar, was a regular visitor. At first Wesley wrote 'The Congregation seemed to understand nothing of the matter but God can give them understanding in his time'. Forty years later he described the village as 'the most fruitful place in all the circuit'. The same vicar's son, Edward Perronet, wrote the hymn *All Hail the power of Jesus' name*. Samuel Palmer, the painter, came here in 1825 to escape London which he described as 'that great national dust hole'. The following year he took up residence at Water House where he was joined by his father and former nurse. Palmer and his friends called themselves the Ancients and often wandered the footpaths at night. Visitors included William Blake who demonstrated clairvoyance by claiming that Palmer was about to enter the house although he had left on the London coach an hour before – Palmer walked in to say the coach had broken down. He described this 'Valley of Vision' as 'near to heaven' and 30 years later he recalled seeing the 'raving mad splendour of orange twilight on landscape at Shoreham'. The woods to the west were familiar to Palmer and the site of Shepherd's Barn, which appears in several of his paintings, is on the north side of Pilots Wood. The 'King's Arms', licensed since 1793, has a well-preserved ostler's box. The stone figure-heads on many of the cottages are believed to come from an 18th-century mansion which stood on the site of Shoreham Place. Filston Hall, to the south, was once home of the Colgate family who later became famous for Colgate toothpaste.

Turn left by the bridge (painted by Palmer) and at 'Ye Old

George Inn' go ahead through the lychgate and up the yew avenue to pass the church. At the far end of the brick path go through the kissing-gate. (*For the station go right and left up the road.*)

Beyond the kissing-gate go left and follow a track to a gateway. Go over the stile at the side and follow an enclosed path to a second stile. Continue ahead along the side of the field to climb over a stile at the end of the field and reach a junction of paths. Turn right to go over a stile and follow the side (right) of the field.

Go over a stile to cross the railway track and walk through an iron kissing-gate. Walk up a short enclosed path to reach the main road. Turn left to pass the entrance (flanked by urns) to the early 19th-century Dunstall Priory (see Shoreham). After a few yards go right up a short stepped path to a gap in the hedge. Bear half left across a field to follow the firm path through a wood. On reaching a clearing keep ahead past a wall and cottage (right) to cross a rough drive and find two footpaths in the corner. Take the left-hand path which climbs up through the trees to become very steep.

At top of the hill keep ahead past a flagpole (see below) and on to the narrow path which runs ahead between the trees (left) and a field to reach a barrier. *If the red flag is flying on the pole (to indicate firing) go right over a stile and follow the diversion signs.* The walk continues ahead through the trees.

On reaching a track go right towards a gateway and then turn left to find a second gateway. Go over the stile and bear half right across a field. On the far side, where the diverted path rejoins, go over a stile and follow a narrow path which runs down the steep wooded hill. The way runs out into the open and bears left along the side of the hill before becoming enclosed and running down to a stile.

Beyond the stile follow the hedge (left) which runs down into a valley. At the bottom turn left to go over a stile by an iron gate and follow a wire fence (right) along the floor of the valley. Cross another stile by a gate and continue following the wire which bears right. On approaching Upper Austin Lodge Farm go over two more stiles to reach a metalled lane.

Turn left to follow the lane for 1¼ miles to Eynsford Station.

On reaching the main road beyond the station turn right and walk down to the village. At the church go left to cross the river and walk past the bottom of Sparepenny Lane.

Just after the road bends go up a bank on the right to pass between stakes by a gate. Follow a footpath half right towards a railway crossing (by a red notice). Cross the line by the stiles and continue quarter right to another stile. Continue forward across a field to reach a metalled road beyond a stile. Turn right and follow the metalled farm road past Hulberry Farm. At a T-junction go half right across the field ahead to reach a barn (or to avoid crops turn right and left on the road). Keep the barn to the left and follow the metalled farm road through Wested Farm to reach a main road.

Turn left along the road to pass the Crocken Hill Football Ground (right). Just beyond Wested Cottage turn right down a narrow enclosed path. The way emerges into the open to follow the side (left) of a field. There are occasional views of Swanley before the path becomes enclosed again and passes Petham Court. The path joins a farm driveway which crosses Swanley by-pass. At a T-junction on the far side of the bridge turn right to follow a road which passes under the railway before reaching a main road. Turn left for the centre of Swanley or right for the bus stop.

11 Along the Mole

LEATHERHEAD — MICKLEHAM DOWNS — BURFORD BRIDGE — BOX HILL —
WEST HUMBLE — MICKLEHAM — LEATHERHEAD
$8\frac{1}{2}$ or 6 MILES

THE COUNTRYSIDE on this circular walk, steeped in literary associations, is largely unspoilt and includes the finest stretch of natural river cliff in the south of England. The area is well served by public transport which enables walkers to break off from the route after only a few miles.

LEATHERHEAD: Bus 265. Green Line Coach 714. London Country Bus 408, 470, 476 (Mondays to Fridays), 478, 479 (Mondays to Saturdays). Or British Rail.

JUNIPER HALL: Green Line Coach 714. London Country Bus 470.

BURFORD BRIDGE and WEST HUMBLE: Green Line Coach 714. London Country Bus 470. British Rail to Boxhill and West Humble.

MICKLEHAM: Green Line Coach 714. London Country Bus 470.

LEATHERHEAD. Many believe the town to be the 'Highbury' in Jane Austen's *Emma*. In Bridge Street there is the 16th-century 'Running Horse' where Eleanor Rumming, the ale-wife in Skelton's poem *The Tunnyng of Elynour Rumming*, kept shop. Judge Jeffreys is believed to have fled to a house in Church Street but, having been betrayed by the butler, escaped through a tunnel to the church of St. Mary & St. Nicholas. The partly Saxon building was founded by Edward the Confessor. Sir Anthony Hope Hawkins (Antony Hope, author of *The Prisoner of Zenda*) is buried in the north-east corner of the churchyard. His father was headmaster of St. John's School. A plaque on the wall of the Mole

Valley District Council offices on Bull Hill records that Kingston House, where John Wesley preached his last sermon in 1791, stood on the site.

Walk along Church Street to pass Leatherhead's parish church (left). Soon the road reaches Gimcrack Hill. At the bottom, beyond Thorncroft Drive (right) go left up Downs Lane. Beyond Vale Lodge Stables (right), the road swings to the right. Later, on reaching Keston Stud, the lane narrows and becomes rough. After swinging left the track runs gently down to the Leatherhead by-pass.

Cross the road to enter Crabtree Drive and at once walk down the bridle-path on the left of the road entrance. The path runs along the back of a garden and gently climbs up into the trees. Ignore a cross path and continue ahead along the enclosed way which occasionally runs out into the open. After passing a cottage (left) the path runs on to cross the entrance to Cherkley Court.

CHERKLEY COURT was the home of Lord Beaverbrook, the statesman and newspaper proprietor, from 1911 until his death here in 1964. He discovered the house whilst out driving with Rudyard Kipling. Cherkley is pronounced locally as 'Charkley' but Beaverbrook insisted on 'Churkley'. His many visitors included Asquith and Bonar Law (who came together as premier and opposition leader to discuss Ireland), Lloyd George, Churchill (who painted the view from the terrace), Lord Bennett (see below), Sir Arthur Bryant and Montgomery. For a time there was a resident orchestra. Beaverbrook also had a private cinema and a direct telephone line to the Daily Express building in Fleet Street.

Keep forward for a short distance and before the way bears left, turn right at a cross-track. (When Bennett had been up to Cherkley for lunch, Beaverbrook would always walk back along this path to his guest's house (see below), and then return home by car.) Follow the track which runs downhill and then up. This is the line of the Roman Stane Street. When the path runs down a short slope go ahead up another slope and bear right along a narrow path which soon joins another path coming from the right).

On reaching an open space keep ahead to join a cross path and bear right. Keep forward (there is an Ordnance triangulation pillar to the right) to follow the path into the trees ahead.

Ignore a turning to the right and keep to the main path known as Downs Road. Soon there is a glimpse (right) of Mickleham Church (see page 80). The way continues through a gateway and runs gently downhill. After passing under a wooden footbridge the track reaches a road. Turn right to walk between Juniper Hill (right) and Juniper Hall (left), to reach a T-junction.

JUNIPER HILL was built about 1780 but reconstructed in 1938 by Richard Bennett who had been the Canadian Prime Minister from 1930 to 1935 and once worked in the same law practice in Canada as Beaverbrook (see above). The empty house was sold to Bennett by Beaverbrook who sent potted plants down from Cherkley to help stock the garden. In 1941 Bennett was made a peer and took the title Viscount Bennett of Mickleham Surrey, and of Calgary and Hopewell, Canada. His butler had been a footman at 10 Downing Street during Asquith's premiership. On Sunday evenings local residents were often invited to view the latest films (sent down from Cherkley). Bennett died here in 1947 and is buried in the churchyard (see page 80).

JUNIPER HALL was rebuilt about 1770 but the outside was altered 100 years later. Following the French Revolution a group of emigrés, including the Count de Narbonne, Talleyrand, Madame de Stael and General D'Arblay, rented the house. When novelist Fanny Burney resigned as Queen Charlotte's second Keeper of the Robes she stayed at nearby Norbury Park and become friendly with D'Arblay who gave her French lessons. They were married (see page 80) in 1793 and after living at Bagdon Hill and Great Bookham moved to West Humble (see page 79). The Hall is now owned by the National Trust and occupied by the Field Studies Council.

Walkers on the shorter route should turn right at the T-junction to reach Mickleham, (see page 81).

The walk continues ahead by the bus stop. Go down the steps by the bus stop and turn left on to the footpath which follows the road (left) south to pass the entrance to Fredley Manor.

FREDLEY MANOR. The 18th-century house was the home of Richard Sharp – the writer, MP and hatmaker who was known as 'Conversation' Sharp. John Stuart Mill (see Mickleham) and his father attended long breakfasts here.

Beyond the manor entrance the path climbs above the road to reach a flight of steps by another bus stop. Continue ahead along the road to reach St. Jude Lodge (left).

A few yards up the lane at the side of St. Jude Lodge is Flint Cottage.

FLINT COTTAGE, built in the early 19th century, was the home of novelist and poet George Meredith from 1867 until his death here in 1909. Each morning he walked to the top of Box Hill and often worked in a chalet in the garden. He was visited by Robert Louis Stevenson (see below) and Henry James. Jeremy Thorpe stayed here as a child when the cottage was owned by his great aunt who gave shelter, during part of the Second World War, to Sir Max and Lady Beerbohm.

To continue the walk cross the top of the lane by St. Jude Lodge and follow the footpath along the bank on the left. The path follows the road (right) for 400 yards before running down to the road by the famous tea stall near the Burford Bridge Hotel.

BURFORD BRIDGE HOTEL, once the 'Fox & Hounds' and later the 'Hare and Hounds', was built in 1800. Nelson, who called it 'a very pretty place', stayed here and is said to have brought Lady Hamilton. In 1817 Keats, escaping from his noisy Hampstead lodgings, spent just over two weeks in a back room overlooking the stable-yard. He had come to finish *Endymion* and on his first night took a moonlit walk up the hill. Byron, Hazlitt, Sheridan and

Young Street Bridge

Leatherhead Church

N

LEATHERHEAD

Cherkley
Court

Mickleham

Juniperhill

Flint Cottage

Burford Bridge
Hotel

Box Hill &
West Humble
Station

Box Hill

Stepping Stones

0   ½   1 mile

Wordsworth also came here. Robert Louis Stevenson stayed twice and wrote part of the *New Arabian Nights* here. Meredith (see above) entertained his friends in the garden. Royal visitors include Queen Victoria who stayed for several days before her accession, Queen Amélie of Portugal had tea here and Queen Alexandra, who also came to tea, said that she had 'never seen a prettier place'. The 15th-century Tithe Barn was brought here in 1934 from Abinger.

Just before the hotel turn left by a bus stop to take a steep path uphill. After a short distance there is a turning to the right – do not take this path (except to view the hotel's garden) but continue uphill. Where the path divides keep right to find an unusual sign-post in the ground. Do not continue to the top of the hill but turn right to follow a narrow but clear path through the trees.

After 200 yards the path runs high above the River Mole. Ignore any turning to the left. The path later meets the river bank just before a footbridge. Continue ahead with the water to reach step-ping stones – part of the ancient Pilgrims' Way.

To visit the Box Hill view turn left into the trees and go right at a cross path. When the rising track levels out, go left on a steep path which later bears right. The way bends and becomes stepped. On reaching a cross path turn right to walk out of the trees. Follow the path round to the left to reach the Box Hill viewpoint.

BOX HILL *is named after the box trees which grew here in great abundance. Sheep are now grazing again to encourage plant and insect life. This was the setting for a picnic in Jane Austen's 'Emma'.*

The walk continues to the right over the stepping stones.

STEPPING STONES. The River Mole, which rises by Gatwick Airport and joins the Thames at Hampton Court, was mentioned by Edmund Spencer, Michael Drayton, John Milton and Alexan-der Pope. When Pope referred to the 'sullen Mole, that hides his driving flood' and Spencer wrote that the river was 'like the mousing mole' who made 'his way still underground till Thames he overtake' they were noting the river's tendency to run under-ground in 'swallow holes' through the chalk – in a period of drought it is possible to walk along the dry river bed whilst the water flows below. The crossing point, now part of the North Downs Way, was re-opened by the then Prime Minister, Clement Attlee, in 1946 when Chuter Ede, the Home Secretary, provided a new set of stones.

Cross the water by the stepping stones and follow the lane ahead. (If the river is running high retrace the path to the foot-bridge). On reaching the main road turn left for a few yards and then cross *with care* the dual carriageway. (To cross the road by a subway turn right on reaching the main road).

Walk up the roughly metalled lane by the bus stop. After 200 yards the way runs under the Leatherhead–Dorking railway line. Keep forward through a gateway. Ignore the first footpath to the right and continue ahead for nearly a quarter mile to turn right on to a narrow cross path which, beyond a stile, runs across a field to a group of houses. Go through a kissing-gate, by a small entrance to 'Pathways', and follow an enclosed narrow path which runs ahead under an apple tree. On reaching a narrow road continue ahead at the side of 'Milton'.

At Chapel Lane turn right and walk down to the junction with Crabtree Lane by St. Michael's chapel and the entrance to Camilla Lacey.

CAMILLA LACEY is a group of houses erected on the site of Camilla Cottage and its garden. The cottage was built in 1796 for Fanny Burney and her husband. He designed the house which was named after Fanny's novel *Camilla* which almost paid for the building. They lived here with their young son until 1807 when D'Arblay returned to France followed by Fanny. Later they were forced to sell the home they loved. The house was destroyed by fire in 1919.

Before the railway bridge (leading to Boxhill & Westhumble Station) go left through the break in the wall to follow an enclosed path down the side of the railway line. Beyond a stile keep ahead along the side of a field to cross the River Mole by a footbridge.

On the far side of the river, walk along the enclosed path. At the end do not turn right under the railway but go over the wooden stile and bear half left across the field towards the white house. On the far side cross a wooden stile and turn right to pass the house (left) and follow a narrow lane. At Cowslip Farm bear right with the lane and after 200 yards pass under the railway.

On the far side of the bridge go left with the road and after a few yards bear half right up a path (by an exposed pipe). The short path leads to the Mickleham by-pass. Cross *with care* the dual carriage-way (built 1934) and continue ahead up an enclosed footpath which passes through a thin belt of trees.

The path bears half left with an overgrown iron fence (right). Beyond the fence there is a clear view of Mickleham Hall. The path continues towards the buildings below the church. At the far end go through a (broken) kissing-gate and turn right on to the unmetalled Swanworth Lane which leads to the village.

MICKLEHAM. The Norman church has been massively restored. Its chancel is slightly offset from the line of the nave and this may be an example of a 'weeping chancel' said to represent the leaning head of Christ on the Cross. In 1793 this was the scene of Fanny Burney's wedding (see page 75), and here George Meredith (see page 76) married his second wife in 1864. Lord Bennett (see page 75), who although a Methodist often read the lessons here, is buried opposite the west door. The sign at the Running Horses shows the 1828 Derby winner, Cadland, who was stabled here and came joint first with The Colonel but won in the re-run between the two. John Stuart Mill, the philosopher, had a summer home here (behind the former Post Office in Swanworth Lane; look for the disused post box behind the clematis) from 1830 to 1857. He sometimes walked along the lanes scattering seeds which he had brought back from France. The village was then an hour's ride by coach from the 'Elephant & Castle' and his guests included Thomas Carlyle.

Turn left by the 'Running Horses' to walk down to the by-pass. *Walkers on the shorter route keep ahead past the 'Running Horses' (left).*

Cross the dual carriageway *with care* and keep ahead to cross the Mole by a bridge. On entering Norbury Park follow the enclosed metalled lane. Ignore a turning to the left and pass Mickleham Priory (right). When the way divides take the left (unmetalled) branch and walk through a wooden gateway.

Follow the track to Lilac Cottage and turn right at a junction of paths. There is a view of Leatherhead church. Follow the trees to a wooden stile by a gate.

Walk through the belt of trees and follow the path which narrows and continues ahead. The river is over to the right. After 400 yards the path reaches a stile by the water. Go ahead under Young Street Bridge.

YOUNG STREET BRIDGE, opened in January 1978 by the Canadian High Commissioner, replaces the Bailey Bridge erected in 1941 by the Royal Canadian Engineers and opened by Mackenzie King – then Canadian Prime Minister who had defeated Richard Bennett in 1935.

After a short distance go over a stile on the river bank and follow the footpath ahead whilst the river swings away to the right. After 300 yards the path runs by a wood (right) and then a wall. Beyond a stile turn right on to Thorncroft Drive. The unmetalled lane soon becomes metalled before passing Thorncroft Manor.

THORNCROFT MANOR was built in 1772 and enlarged about 1800. Colonel Drinkwater Bethune, who wrote the history of the seige of Gibraltar (1779–83), lived here.

The road crosses the Mole to reach a main road. Turn left up Gimcrack Hill to walk into Leatherhead.

12 Surrey Valleys

CATERHAM – CHALDON – COULSDON COMMON – WADDINGTON –
KENLEY COMMON – WHYTELEAFE – WARLINGHAM – WOLDINGHAM –
CATERHAM
$5\frac{1}{2}$ or $11\frac{1}{4}$ MILES

THIS IS a hilly circular walk over some of Surrey's finest commons served conveniently by a red bus route.

CATERHAM: Bus 197. London Country Bus 409 (Mondays to Saturdays), 411 (Mondays to Saturdays), 411A (Sundays). Or British Rail.

COULSDON COMMON: London Country Bus 409 (Mondays to Saturdays), 411 (Mondays to Saturdays), 411a (Sundays). Or bus 190 from Old Coulsdon.

WHYTELEAFE: Bus 115 (Mondays to Fridays), 197. Or British Rail.

WARLINGHAM: London Country Bus 403, 453, 483 (Mondays to Saturdays).

WOLDINGHAM: London Country Bus 440 (Mondays to Saturdays). Or British Rail.

CATERHAM was a small village until 1856 when the railway arrived in the valley. St. Mary's, at the top of the hill, was built in 1866 to succeed the Norman parish church opposite. Its 13th-century font is now in St. John's (near the station). Upwood Gorse, in Upwood Lane, was built for Queen Victoria's dentist.

Leave the bus stop or station and walk up Church Hill. Just beyond the two churches and Manor Avenue (the former entrance to the Manor House) go left at a bus stop to follow an enclosed path into Queen's Park. The metalled path runs along the edge of the park and, beyond a barrier, runs parallel to a lane before running downhill to Roffes Lane.

Cross Roffes Lane and go ahead up The Heath. Turn right into Chaldon Common Road. On meeting Rook Lane, go left and on Rook Hill (ahead) go right through an iron gate to follow an enclosed path. After ⅓ mile the path meets a residential road. Turn left and keep right where the road divides. Just before the road bends, go right on to a rough track. After a few yards turn left to walk down the side of Piles Wood (right). Keep ahead where the trees end to reach Church Lane. Turn right to pass the entrances (left) to Chaldon Church.

CHALDON comes from 'Chalvedune' meaning 'calves down'. The church is 11th-century with an Early English south aisle. The famous wall painting (discovered in 1869 when decorators were washing the west wall) was created about 1200, possibly by a monk. The lower half of the work depicts Hell and on the ladder there are souls climbing to Heaven. The rare pulpit is Cromwellian. The spire was added in 1842.

After a few yards turn right to turn into a field. Follow a path half left across the field. After ¼ mile the path passes between two woods and runs down to a belt of trees. Walk through the trees to cross a wooden stile.

Follow the hedge (right) across Happy Valley to walk up the stepped path opposite. At the top turn right on to a rough path which bears left and becomes metalled. Follow the straight path and at the end go through a wooden gate to pass the 'Fox' (right) and reach a main road at Coulsdon Common.

COULSDON COMMON. Old Coulsdon lies to the north of the Common. The 13th-century church (at the north end of the main road) was enlarged in 1958. The Barn, on the west side of Bradmore Green, and Taunton Farmhouse, in Taunton Lane, both date from the 16th century. Caterham Barracks, home of the Guards, is to the south of the Common.

Cross the road to enter Coulsdon Common. Where the metalled path ends, continue ahead on the rough path which bears round to the left through the trees. On meeting a road (Stites Hill) go ahead down Rydon's Lane.

At the end of Rydon's Lane go over Caterham Drive and up a steep footpath (known as Waterhouse Lane). At the top turn left at once to walk through the trees. After 400 yards the path turns away from the edge and runs out into the open by a cottage (left). Follow the lane ahead and turn right with the way as it becomes metalled. Another farm path joins from the left before the main path meets Old Lodge Lane.

Turn right along the lane and go left by the 'Wattenden Arms'. The path runs past several buildings to reach a barrier. Beyond the barrier bear right to follow a path to Hayes Lane. Go right along the lane and then left (by the phone and post box) to walk up Golf Road.

At the end of the rough road go through a gateway to enter Kenley Common. Keep to the footpath on the right which soon runs past the end of a Kenley Aerodrome runway (right). Do not bear right beyond the runway but go forward to join a path (known as Stumps Lane) running downhill through the wood. When the steep path meets a metalled road go ahead across two junctions to follow a footpath over a railway line and reach God-stone Road (by a bus stop for Bus 197) at Whyteleafe.

Turn right and then left to walk up Maple Road. Go under the railway bridge and keep forward to follow the trees (left). On coming level with the tennis courts (right) turn left into the trees to follow a steep path up the side of the hill. At the top the path runs into the open and across a field to meet a road.

Go left for a few yards and then right (before a school) to enter Batts Farm. Beyond the row of Victorian cottages turn right to walk up the side (right) of the cottages. On reaching a playing field

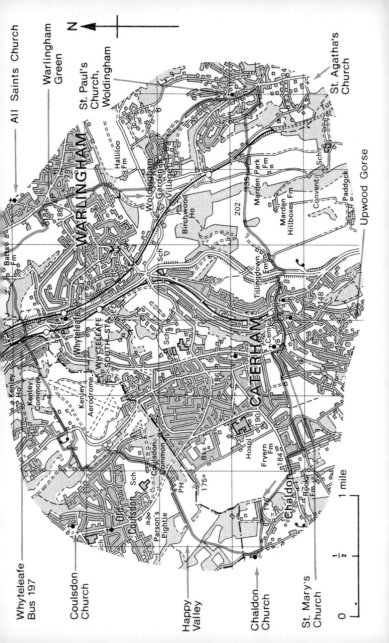

keep to the right and at a line of trees ahead turn left and then right
to enter the next field and continue southwards. Beyond a cross
path keep ahead with the side (left) of the field. At the far end of the
field continue ahead up an enclosed path to reach the entrance to
the Eagle Star Sports Ground. Keep forward up the short residential road to meet a main road. Turn right to reach Warlingham.

WARLINGHAM. All Saints' Church dates from about 1250. The
font is 15th-century and on the north side there is a wall painting of
St. Christopher carrying Christ. Archbishop Cranmer, staying at
Croydon Palace, is said to have been present when his prayer book
was used here as an experiment in 1549. The Vicarage, in Westhall
Road, was built in the 17th century along with the nearby Atwood
Almshouses (see below).

Walk past 'Ye Olde Leather Bottle' and continue past the Green
(left) to enter Westhall Road (by a garage on the right). At once
bear half left into Leas Road. On the corner of Chapel Road (left)
there are the Atwood Almshouses and on the right there is grass.
Keep ahead along Leas Road to reach the top of Bug Hill.

Leave the road (by Tydcombe Road) by bearing half left off the
road and down a woodland path. Do not turn left before the house
but keep ahead at the side of the house (right) to reach a stile on the
edge of the wood. Below is Halliloo Farm.

Climb over the stile and bear half right down the hill to cross
another stile. Continue half right towards the house in the distance.
Climb over a stile opposite the house and cross the road.

Do not go up the rough road ahead but turn half left up the
metalled drive. Beyond the Coach House (right) the way becomes
rough and steeper. At the top of the hill cross a road (leading to
Woldingham Garden Village – a former First World War army
camp), to keep ahead up a narrow path by a modern building (left).
The path later passes a solitary house (right) and where the way
divides keep left on the higher path. Below (right) there is a view

across a valley. After ½ mile the path runs beside a garden and down to join Long Hill.

Turn left up the rough lane which runs gently up hill and round a bend to Woldingham Church.

WOLDINGHAM The tiny flint church of St. Agatha, built in 1832 on the site of a pre 14th-century church, still stands at the end of Church Road. St. Paul's was built in 1933 in memory of the first Earl of Inchcape who had died in 1932. The present rector is the distinguished Canon Douglas Rhymes whose recreations include country walking.

Continue past the church (left) and shops (left) to go right, by the green, down Park View Road. Follow the road which, after 250 yards, bears right. Turn left off the road between Haverback and The Red Cottage (left) to walk down a long stepped path. Cross a stile at the end and continue forward downhill to pass between two trees. Go over a stile and cross Church Road to follow a path (almost opposite) over the railway line. At once turn right with the fenced path and at the corner go left up a short avenue to go through an iron gate.

Keep ahead between the buildings of Marden Park Farm. Bear right and left to follow the drive down to a lane. Cross the road and go over a stile between two wooden gates. Climb up the steep enclosed path to walk through a strip of woodland (known as The Bushes) and reach a stile and gate. Keep ahead near a fence (left) and go over the brow of the hill to cross another stile. Follow the way which runs gently downhill to pass a barn (left) hidden in a wood. Ahead there is a view of the Caterham Church spire. Climb over a wooden stile to look across a valley to Tillingdown Farm.

Go ahead downhill and climb the farm track on the opposite side to reach Tillingdown Farm. The path runs through the farmyard. Follow a lane ahead which soon bears left to run above the Caterham by-pass. After 200 yards bear right on to a track and

at once go left over a bank to find a short path which leads to a flight
of steps. Go down the steps and cross *with care* the dual carriageway.

Follow a narrow footpath which runs into the trees. Where the
way divides bear left down a long stepped path. At the road keep
ahead down Timber Hill Road to reach the centre of Caterham.

13 Over the Hill

ELTHAM – SHOOTER'S HILL – PLUMSTEAD COMMON – LESNES ABBEY
6 MILES

THIS WALK, never far from a bus route, crosses Shooter's Hill which
has been a gateway to London since Roman times. This rural walk
recalls a time when the area was part of the 'Garden of England'.

ELTHAM: Bus 21, 21A, 61, 108, 124, 124A (Sundays), 126, 132,
160, 161, 161A (Mondays to Saturdays), 228, B1 (Mondays to
Saturdays). Green Line Coach 729 (Mondays to Fridays). Or British Rail to Eltham Well Hall.

SHOOTER'S HILL: Bus 89, 192.

SHREWSBURY LANE: Bus 192.

PLUMSTEAD COMMON: Bus 51, 53.

WICKHAM LANE: Bus 53 (Sundays), 96, 122, 122A.

BOSTALL HEATH ROAD: Bus 99.

LESNES ABBEY: Bus 177, 180, 269, 272. Or British Rail.

ELTHAM. The Palace was a Royal home from Edward IV to
Charles I. In 1400 Henry IV was married by proxy in the chapel –

the site has recently been excavated. Henry V returned here after his triumph at Agincourt. Here, during Christmas 1515, Cardinal Wolsey was made Lord Chancellor by Henry VIII. In 1556 Mary I's Privy Council met here to discuss the defence of Calais. Much of the Palace was destroyed by the Roundheads and Edward IV's hall, which has the third largest hammerbeam roof in England, became a barn. The Great Hall is now open on Thursdays and Saturdays 10 30 to 12 30 and 14 15 to 18 00 (16 00 November to February); admission free. The 18th-century 'Greyhound' (in the High Street) has two 16th-century fireplaces which may have come from the Palace. Thomas Doggett, the founder of Doggett's Coat and Badge Race, is buried outside the south wall of St. John's Church. Herbert Morrison, the Foreign Secretary, lived at 55 Archery Road from 1929 to 1960. Rex Whistler, the artist, was born nearby in Passey Place.

Leave the High Street and walk north up Well Hall Road to go under the railway and reach Well Hall (left).

WELL HALL PLEASAUNCE was the house of Margaret Roper, daughter of St. Thomas More – hence the church of St. John Fisher and St. Thomas More to the north. The Roper's house was replaced by an 18th-century building (now demolished) which, in 1899, became the home of E. Nesbit, who wrote *The Railway Children* here, and her husband Hubert Bland, who helped to found the Fabian Society. Their visitors included G. K. Chesterton, E. M. Forster, Laurence Housman and Bernard Shaw – H. G. Wells wrote '. . . one rushed down from town at the weekend to snatch one's bed before anyone else got it'. In the local paper E. Nesbit advertised 'new laid eggs' as being on sale at Well Hall 'opposite the Co-operative Stores'. The farmyard is now grassed and only the moat, rose garden walls and barn remain from the Tudor house. The gallery in the barn is open daily except Saturday, 11 00 to 20 00 hours (to dusk September to March) and on the ground floor of the barn morning coffee and lunches are served daily except Sunday. The bell is mentioned in E. Nesbit's *The Would-begoods*. Bop Hope was born at 44 Craighton Road (opposite Well Hall).

On reaching Well Hall (left) turn right up Dunvegan Road. At the far end of the road go ahead to enter Eltham Park. The path runs gently uphill and across an open space. To the left there is a view across South London to the Crystal Palace. On the far side of the open space go ahead on to a rough path which runs into Shepherdleas Wood and bears half right. Soon the way bends left to reach a junction of paths.

Go half right (and not ahead or right) on to a narrow path to pass a seat (right). Keep on the winding path and on meeting a cross-path at a T-junction turn left. Ignore all turnings and bear right with the path to reach, beyond a firm cross path, a main road.

Cross the road to enter the woods (by the 'Welling' sign). The traffic lights to the right often provide an easier crossing point. Go over the grass ride and cross the footbridge to reach a track by a small car park (right). Turn left to follow the track (Crown Woods Lane) away from the car park and into Oxleas Wood.

Pass the top of a wide avenue (right) and keep ahead on the path which runs uphill between the wood (right) and a metalled path (left). At the top of the hill walk over to a tearoom where there is a magnificent view across south-east London.

Go behind the tearoom to follow an enclosed metalled lane (the continuation of Crown Woods Lane) which runs northwards. On reaching new houses at Kenilworth Gardens bear right to the main road on the top of Shooter's Hill.

SHOOTER'S HILL is part of the Roman Watling Street and the pilgrim road to Canterbury. From here many foreign visitors enjoyed their first view of London. Pepys mentions the hill in his diary for 1661 and in *Don Juan* Byron tells of a hold-up here. In *A*

Tale of Two Cities Dickens described the Dover Mail lumbering up the hill in November 1775 with the passengers plodding along in the mud. The mounting stone indicates the position of the original 'Bull' which was very fashionable in the 18th century. Schoolboy Paul Nash (see page 13) went on cross-country runs involving the 'interminable Shooters Hill'.

Turn left and then right (by the 'Bull') to walk along Shrewsbury Lane. Between the houses on the left there are views across London with St. Paul's Cathedral and the Post Office Tower usually clearly visible. Beyond the fire station (right) and the tumulus (left) the road becomes Plum Lane. As the road begins to run downhill follow the right hand pavement which swings into Shrewsbury Park.

SHREWSBURY PARK was once the grounds of (the now demolished) Shrewsbury House. On the opposite side of Plum Lane there was (until the 1930s) Tower House, home of philanthropist Lord Teynham and from 1897 Edward Jay, father of former cabinet minister Douglas Jay (who spent his childhood here) and grandfather of ex-ambassador Peter Jay.

Follow the main path through the Park to pass a car park (left) and a tea hut (right). The path continues past a wood (left) and an open space. Ahead there is a fine view across Welling and northeast Kent. Beyond a shelter (left) follow the path which runs steeply downhill to cross a rough lane.

The unmetalled footpath ahead soon gives way to grass. To the right there is a view over Plumstead to Bostall Woods (see page 93) and to the left there is, after a short distance, a view of Woolwich and the Thames. Keep forward to take a flight of steps which leads down to the top of Upton Road.

Walk down Upton Road and opposite Olven Road (left) go right down a short flight of steps. At the bottom turn right along Ennis Road to reach the 'Ship' at Plumstead Common.

N

Lesnes Abbey

Abbey Wood Station

Plumstead Common Windmill

Shrewsbury Park

'The Bull;
Shooters Hill

St. John Fisher &
St. Thomas More Church

Well Hall

Eltham Palace

0   ½   1 mile

PLUMSTEAD COMMON is the high ground of Plumstead. The former fishing village is on the side of the hill and at high tide the Thames used to reach almost to the 12th-century church of St. Nicholas in St. Nicholas Road. The 'Volunteer' in the High Street was once the parsonage. The 'Plume of Feathers' dates from the 18th century. Until 100 years ago the village was famous for its Kent apple orchards. The 'Old Mill' incorporates the remains of a windmill and has been a pub since flour grinding ceased in 1848.

Cross the road and bear half right down Windmill Road (with the avenue of trees). Go ahead at the cross roads to pass the 'Old Mill' (left).

Continue along Old Mill Road to pass Plumstead Manor School (left) and the 'Prince Albert'. Before reaching the modern church of St. Mary with St. Margaret bear half right (opposite Chestnut Rise) to follow a metalled path to the top of a flight of steps. Go down the steps to pass a pond (right) and climb more steps. At the top go ahead across two roads and walk over to join the main road (on the right). Beyond the bus stop, do not go downhill with the main road, but keep ahead on a lane (whilst the main road swings away to the right).

On reaching an old car yard go down the steps on the right which lead back to the main road. On joining the road keep ahead past the 'Alma' to a cross roads by London Transport's Plumstead Bus Garage.

Cross Wickham Lane and go ahead up Waterdale Road towards Bostall Woods. At the end keep forward up the slope and steps to a cross path. Go right and, after a short distance, turn left up a valley to follow a wooden water duct (right). Where the duct ends leave the rising path to bear sharp right on a hairpin bend and find another rising path. The way bears left to run along the wooded cliff before bearing left again up a valley. On reaching a junction of paths turn left and left again on to a path which rises out of the trees and becomes metalled.

Beyond a circular seat (round a tree) leave the path and bear half right between the tree (right) and a building (left) to reach a road by a bowling green (right).

Cross the road and pass between a garden (left) and a car park (right) and head towards a belt of trees. Beyond the trees go left across Clam Field to cross Bostall Hill Road and follow an un-metalled drive (lined with low posts). On meeting a cross drive, near a house (left), keep ahead to a road. Turn left on to Knee Hill and then right into Hurst Lane.

On reaching an iron barrier (left and opposite a turning into Hurst Park Estate) go left through the barrier to follow a path through Lesnes Abbey Woods. The way bears slightly right and then slightly left before beginning a gentle run downhill – passing a fenced pond (right). At the bottom of the hill bear right with the path and ignore all turnings. The way runs past several back gardens (left) before reaching a short flight of steps and a road.

Cross the road to follow a path which runs between the wood (right) and a park. When the fence (left) gives way to a hedge keep on the path. At a second gap turn left into the park and walk towards the Abbey ruins.

LESNES ABBEY was founded in 1178 by Richard de Lucy (see page 44) as an act of penance for being involved in the murder of St. Thomas à Becket. The abbey was suppressed by Cardinal Wolsey more than ten years before Henry VIII began his dissolution pro-gramme. Although this was an Augustinian community it was built to a Cistercian plan and about twelve monks lived here. The daffodils which flower on the hill are believed by some to be wild descendants of bulbs planted 800 years ago by the monks.

Keep to the left of the ruins to follow a path to a bridge where steps lead down to Abbey Road and bus stops.

14 Three Royal Parks

WHITEHALL – ST. JAMES'S PARK – GREEN PARK – HYDE PARK –
KENSINGTON GARDENS
3 MILES

WILLIAM III considered Kensington Palace to be a country retreat
outside London. Today it is still possible to take the 3-mile rural
walk, preserved by the Royal Parks, from Whitehall to the Royal
Borough of Kensington.

WHITEHALL: Underground to Charing Cross (Bakerloo,
Jubilee and Northern Lines), Embankment (Bakerloo, Circle, Dis-
trict and Northern Lines) or Westminster (Circle and District
Lines).

HYDE PARK CORNER: Underground (Piccadilly line).

KENSINGTON HIGH STREET: Underground to High Street
Kensington (Circle and District lines).

Leave Whitehall by walking through the Horse Guards Arch
(opposite the Banqueting House).

HORSE GUARDS was designed by William Kent and built in the
1750s. The Life Guards are normally on duty here at the military
headquarters flanked by government buildings. Opposite is the
17th-century Banqueting House – almost the only remains of
Whitehall Palace. In 1649 Charles I passed through a now blocked
up window (above the door) to his execution. Here in 1660 Parlia-
ment assembled to welcome Charles II and in 1688 to offer the
Crown to William and Mary. The Banqueting House, which has a
magnificent Rubens ceiling commissioned by Charles I, is open
Tuesdays to Sundays 10 00 (14 00 Sundays) to 17 00; admission
30p, children and pensioners 15p.

Beyond the arch there is Horse Guards Parade.

HORSE GUARDS PARADE is on the site of the Whitehall Palace tiltyard. Here the Queen's Birthday Parade (Trooping the Colour) and Beating Retreat ceremonies take place.

Keep to the right of the Guards' Memorial ahead and enter St. James's Park.

ST JAMES'S PARK was first enclosed by Henry VIII when he seized the land belonging to Westminster Abbey. Under Charles II the pools were made into a canal by Le Nôtre whose work the King had seen during his exile in France. The canal was turned into the present ornamental water by John Nash in 1825. The pelicans have been here since one was presented to Charles II by the Russian Ambassador. Birdcage Walk, on the south side, takes its name from Charles' aviary which stood on the edge of the Park.

Follow the path ahead to pass the Cake House (right) and then the lake (left), to reach the bridge. The path to the right leads to St. James's Palace.

ST. JAMES'S PALACE was the main royal home from the 16th century until Victoria's early decision to use Buckingham Palace. Ambassadors are still accredited to the Court of St. James's. Charles II, James I, the Old Pretender, Mary II, Queen Anne and George IV were all born here. In the west side there is Clarence House, the Queen Mother's house.

The walk continues ahead. On reaching a high wall, at the end of the Park, leave the water and turn right to reach The Mall. To the left there is a clear view of Buckingham Palace.

BUCKINGHAM PALACE was built early in the 18th century as Buckingham House for the Duke of Buckingham. In 1761 it became Queen Charlotte's home, a retreat from St. James's Palace. Nash built a new house around the original structure and George

IV declared 'It will make an excellent Palace'. Three weeks after her accession Queen Victoria became the first monarch to take up residence. The front was added in 1847 but given a new façade in 1913. The Chinese Luncheon Room (at the right hand end) incorporates parts of Brighton Pavilion's Banqueting and Music Rooms. The Queen's office, Audience Chamber and private apartments overlook Constitution Hill. The Royal Standard, which is the only flag to be flown from the mast, signifies that Her Majesty is in residence although not necessarily at home. The Queen's Gallery, where part of the Royal Art collection is on show, is open daily, except Mondays, 11 00 (14 00 Sundays) to 17 00, admission 60p (children, students and pensioners 25p). The Royal Mews is open on Wednesdays and Thursdays 14 00 to 16 00; admission 25p (children, students and pensioners 10p).

Across The Mall, half right, there is a glimpse of Lancaster House.

LANCASTER HOUSE described as the 'most palatial private residence in Europe', was built in 1825 for the Duke of York (of nursery rhyme fame). Wyatt was chosen as architect after Samuel Smirke had quarrelled with the Duke, but on his death, Smirke added the attic. In 1850 the Queen and Prince Albert came to hear Chopin and Victoria told her hostess, the Duchess of Sutherland, 'I have come from my home to your palace.' The Jubilee Year Commonwealth Prime Ministers Conference was held here and in 1979 the house was the venue for the Rhodesian Constitutional Conference. Open Summer Saturdays and Sundays 14 00 to 18 00; admission 50p, children and pensioners 25p.

Cross The Mall and go ahead to follow the balustrade (left) round to the left. On reaching a gateway (left) turn right into Green Park.

GREEN PARK once known as Upper St. James's Park, was made into a park at the request of Charles II in 1667. Constitution Hill, to the south, recalls the King's regular morning walks. A shallow valley marks the line of the now underground River Tyburn and the grass banks are the remains of defences thrown up by Cromwell. Queen's Walk, on the east side, is named after Queen Caroline, wife of George II. The gates at the top of the main walk once stood at the entrance to the now demolished Devonshire House – opposite the Ritz.

Turn left at the second turning and at a junction of paths keep forward ignoring two turnings to the left. The path runs across the gentle valley and the grass mounds and runs up to the edge of Piccadilly. At the top of the Park go through a small gate and cross the road by the subway. To the left is Wellington Arch.

WELLINGTON ARCH was designed by Decimus Burton and erected in 1846. The figure of Peace in a chariot replaced an equestrian statue of Wellington (now in Aldershot) in 1912 as a tribute to Edward VII.

Walk past the Machine Gun Corps Memorial (right) and go under the next subway (right). In emerging from the tunnel bear right to pass the front of Apsley House.

APSLEY HOUSE is known as 'No. 1 London' – it was the first beyond the turnpike. The Duke of Wellington bought the late 18th-century house from Baron Apsley in 1817, two years after the Battle of Waterloo, and Wyatt transformed it. The 90 foot gallery was added for the Waterloo Day dinners. The house is now the Wellington Museum and contains a display of the 'Iron Duke's' decorations. Open Tuesdays to Saturdays 10 00 to 18 00 and Sundays 14 30 to 18 00; admission free.

Beyond Apsley House turn right to go through the Hyde Park Corner Screen to enter Hyde Park.

HYDE PARK was part of the Westminster Abbey estate until 1536 when it was seized by Henry VIII. James I opened the area to the public, who, except during the Cromwellian period, have had

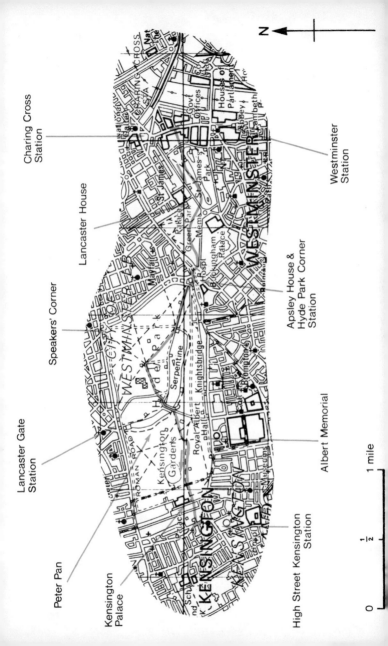

access ever since. George III was the last monarch to hunt here. Rotten Row, where Lillie Langtry later rode with the 'Langtry Lancers', was originally 'La Route du Roi' which ran from St. James's Palace to William III's new country palace in Kensington and in the winter the road was lit by 300 oil lamps – the first street lighting. George II's wife, Caroline, had the Westbourne stream turned into the Long Water and Serpentine. In the 18th century the Powder Magazine was placed in the centre of the Park in case there was a gunpowder accident – the present exterior was remodelled by Decimus Burton in about 1825. The Great Exhibition was held in the Crystal Palace which stood just south of the Serpentine. George Lansbury was responsible for introducing the Serpentine Lido – before 1930 swimming was restricted to early morning and males. Skating is allowed if the ice is 5 inches thick. An illegal public meeting in 1855 led to the creation of Speakers' Corner in 1872. The Hyde Park Corner Screen was designed by Decimus Burton in 1825. Amid all the changes wildlife remains and over 90 bird species have been seen in the Park.

Walk down the side of Apsley House. Cross the wide road ahead and bear half left, not to enter the sandy Rotten Row, but to follow Serpentine Road (which has a narrow ride at the side).

After a short distance there is the Cavalry Memorial and bandstand (right). On reaching the Dell Restaurant (left), on the edge of the Serpentine, bear half right on to a path which leads away from the road. After just over ¼ mile the path reaches the Hyde Park Police Station. Walk down the side of the Police Station and before reaching a road the wide path passes (right) Epstein's *Rima* (see page 52).

At the road go left to follow the road around a double bend to pass the colonnaded Powder Magazine (right) and cross the Serpentine by the Bridge (built in 1826) which marks the boundary between the Long Water (right) and the Serpentine (left).

On the far side of the water turn right to go through a gateway and enter Kensington Gardens.

KENSINGTON GARDENS was the garden of Kensington
Palace and George II's Queen Caroline did much to improve the
landscape – elms (which lasted until 1953) were planted according
to the position of troops at the Battle of Blenheim. Under the
Hanovarians the Gardens were open on Saturday when Court was
away and early in Victoria's reign the Gardens were open 'all the
year round to all respectably dressed persons, from sunrise to
sunset'. In 1815 Shelley's first wife drowned in the Long Water.
The Pumping Station at the top of the Long Water is said to have
been designed by Prince Albert and based on the Petit Trianon at
Versailles. J. M. Barrie, who lived at 100 Bayswater Road, paid for
Sir George Frampton's *Peter Pan* statue and presented the swings in
the playground. The Elfin Oak is an 800 year old oak stump from
Richmond Park – the elves and animals were carved by Ivor Innes
in the 1930s and restored in 1966 by Spike Milligan. The statue of
Physical Energy, by G. F. Watts, is a bronze cast of the original in
Cape Town.

*To reach Lancaster Gate Underground Station go right to follow the
Long Water. Beyond the Peter Pan statue and the Fountains, go through
the gate to find the station across Bayswater Road.*

The walk continues on the path ahead. The Serpentine Gallery is
to the left. As the path crosses Lancaster Walk there is a view of
Physical Energy (right) and the Albert Memorial (left).

ALBERT MEMORIAL, completed in 1872 at a cost of £120,000,
was designed by Sir George Gilbert Scott, who described it as 'a
kind of ciborium . . . to protect a statue'. Prince Albert is holding a
copy of the Great Exhibition catalogue.

Keep forward and after passing the bandstand (right) take a path
to the right which leads up to the Broad Walk, near the Round
Pond (right) – a pool converted by George I.

Go ahead, across the Broad Walk, and down a steep slope, to
follow a wide path along the side of Kensington Palace.

KENSINGTON PALACE dates from 1605. William III and Mary moved here from central London in 1689 because of the King's asthma and called in Wren to enlarge the house. Both monarchs died here. Queen Anne, who also died here, made it her country home and added the Orangery – the architect was probably Hawksmoor, Wren's assistant. George I and II used the Palace and the latter, who had made it his permanent home, died here awaiting news from Hanover – his ghost has been reported watching the wind-dial in the King's Gallery for a fair wind from Germany. George III, who preferred Windsor and Kew, gave his son, the Duke of Kent, an apartment here. Kent's daughter, Queen Victoria, was born here in 1819 and baptized in the Cupola Room – on a visit 82 years later she insisted that she had never been in the room! At the ceremony her father and the Prince Regent could not agree on names and, when her mother's name was suggested as a compromise, the Archbishop quickly christened the child 'Victoria'. She grew up here and became Queen 18 years later whilst asleep in the King's State Bed Chamber – her toys and dolls' house are in the ante-room. (The statue of Victoria, opposite the Round Pond is by her daughter, Princess Louise). Queen Mary was born in Victoria's former bedroom in 1867. Mary's mother, the Duchess of Teck, ran up huge bills in the local shops and caused a stir at the opening of a hall, built partly with a donation from John Barker (of Barkers shop) by proposing a special vote of thanks to Mr. Barker to whom we all owe so much'. Part of the Palace is now occupied by Princess Margaret, the Duke and Duchess of Gloucester, Princess Alice Duchess of Gloucester and Princess Alice Countess of Athlone, who is Queen Victoria's granddaughter. The State Apartments are open daily 09 00 (13 00 Sundays) to 17 00. Admission 60p; children and pensioners 30p (40p and 20p October to March).

Keep forward to leave Kensington Gardens and cross Palace Avenue (which leads to the Royal entrance to the Palace) and reach a second road, Kensington Palace Gardens.

KENSINGTON PALACE GARDENS, known as Millionaires' Row, is built on the site of the Palace's kitchen garden. When the advent of the railways in the 1840s enabled produce to be brought swiftly from Windsor then the land was laid out as a street. Over the next 20 years large houses, some Italianate, were built. 2 Palace Green (as the south end is known) was designed by Thackeray for himself at a cost of more than £8,000 shortly before his death in 1863. Most of the houses have been preserved as embassy residences – 10, 16 and 18 Kensington Palace Gardens are occupied by the Russian Embassy.

Cross the road to follow the narrow York House Place which leads to Kensington Church Street.

The bus stops are to the right. To reach High Street Kensington Station go left and then right, opposite Barkers, into Kensington High Street.

INDEX